the
babes' bible

graphics
Richard Rockwood

dedication
To the men in our lives who
inspire us: for Raff and Paul
with love.

the babes' bible

**Elizabeth Hearn and
Sada Walkington**

Quadrille

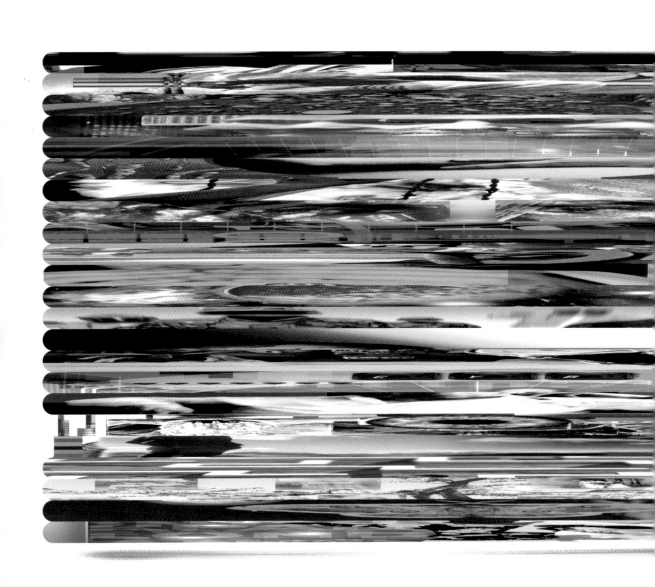

contents

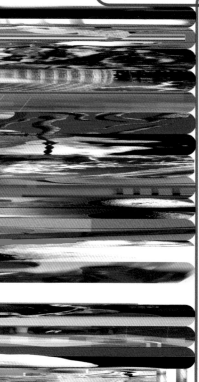

preface

Are you struggling in the singles zone? Do you really know who you are sleeping with? How often have you made the wrong choice? Or been surprised or disappointed when he didn't measure up to your expectations? And, if you're in a relationship now, do you understand what makes your man tick?

Success in the dating and mating game comes down to finding the right 'type' – the guy you are best suited to, the one you're compatible with at this particular time in your life. But how do you recognize him and, once you've hooked him, how do you keep him?

The Babes' Bible is a light-hearted look into a serious subject, a reality-check rooted in the dynamics that motivate men today. We have jumped fearlessly into the male psyche and come back with 24 personality profiles based on the ancient archetypes to represent the spectrum of the contemporary male. We have connected the dots and bridged the gap between the sexes to provide you with insight into the way he sees himself, his world and his relationships.

If you've ever been frustrated by men's silence, their sheer disinclination to communicate – and let's face it, who hasn't? – this is the book for you. It's both a guide designed to help you to recognize the various types that exist out there so you're better

equipped to find the right man for you and a maintenance manual that aims to explain his angle on the interactive game of relationships.

So, if you want to make the most out of love, relax, pour yourself a bath and take the night off. You are about to discover the ancient secrets that drive modern men.

understanding the
modern male

In the past, societies all over the world classified people according to their drives and motivations. The myths and legends of practically every culture contain characters with specific defining traits that override the restrictions of social stereotyping. You can find these archetypes, as they are called, in fairytales, in religion, and even in mainstream cinema today.

Take a look at Hollywood's no.1 action man – an adaptation of the mythological hero archetype. He wears the same macho-muscle T-shirt throughout the film. He shoots first and asks questions later. He'll be roughed up, but by the time the credits roll he's saved the world, won over the resistant babe *and* found time to feed the dog.

Thousands of years ago the masculine role was clear: in tribal society men had to rely on their instincts and strengths to survive. Anthropologists have concluded that one man, the village chief, was seen as the embodiment of the characteristics of all the ancient archetypes. The chief was King, Warrior, Magician, Altruist, Lover, Hero, Innocent and Wanderer. As such he was the ultimate leader – the prophet and seer, all-knowing, a divine counsellor and keeper of the key. He was supported by the elders, whose responsibility it was to raise the boys of the village to become strong warriors possessing heroic qualities.

Each boy would be guided by the elders through the various stages that marked his journey from birth through boyhood to manhood. He would receive lessons in the sacred teachings to secure his safe passage through the trials of ritual and initiation that prepared him for the rigours of adult life. And he would be told the tribal stories to keep the ancestral beliefs alive. This passing on of wisdom would fire the boy's imagination and define his destiny. His life was shaped by those who had much to offer from hard-won experience.

Today a new challenge awaits young boys as they reach adolescence. If present, his father will have taken him as far as he can, but the village chief and the elders are long gone. If the boy is fortunate, he may have relatives or close family friends who can take on a part of their role. But he is no longer afforded the opportunity of structured initiation into a composite identity drawn from the available male archetypes.

He is without doubt the Innocent Warrior, and he must discover the other roles open to him alone. No longer equipped with ancestral teachings to aid his progress into manhood, he must learn from what is available. He will be influenced by his surroundings and his role models. He will find heroes in computer war games, comics, videos or cinematic epics. He will seek out role models for the values of trust, wisdom, co-operation and communion.

Everybody needs a hero, and for the young boy this need represents his longing for the idealized father. He will attach himself to the man he most wants to become. That choice is often made when a significant event fires his imagination – he may identify with a national sporting hero or he may choose to follow in his father's footsteps. This need to identify with a masculine role model is essential. This is how he will learn from men, by observing and internalizing his hero's journey in life. His adolescent years represent his rites of passage and what he derives from aspects of his 'tribe' will influence his emerging masculine identity. He will develop his life course, which will define his role and life purpose. And so the boy evolves into the man, using his dominant archetype to pursue what he wants from life.

That's the theory. In practice, we believe, most men are a complex tangle of archetypal aspects. A dominant archetype will govern his thinking and his heart. But life's experiences of transition and transformation can re-connect him to secondary archetypes. In fatherhood, for example, the Warrior has the opportunity to re-connect to his Innocent archetype.

Or imagine a young man forced by a dictatorial father to abandon his plans for film school. His Lover archetype is repressed and he goes instead into corporate banking. He prospers and for a time those boyhood ideals are forgotten. Then comes the day when he just doesn't want to perform the role of the city warrior any longer.

Something is missing from his existence, but what? He's got the capital, the babe, the corner office, but emotionally he's functioning on auto-pilot. He has forgotten how to have fun, and he thinks he's lost his purpose. So he calls a guy he met at the last corporate training weekend, a calm, clear-thinking man, able to listen without judgment.

Sadly, however, it is often less problematic for a man to fake an everything-is-fine façade. We live in a time when there is enormous pressure on men in particular to be strong and 'sorted'. It's all the more remarkable, then, that many men recognize the need to work towards enlightened, expressive, insightful and respectful ways of interacting with other men and with women. Twenty-first century men want understanding and loving relationships with women, so it's time for women to accept men for who they are. We need to meet them halfway. And that's not easy – everything has changed so much in the game of love. Men's anxieties have left women equally disconcerted and bemused. Essentially there are no rules anymore. We need to listen to one another. We need to be real.

our contemporary archetypes

The psychoanalyst Carl Jung, influenced by the work of the mythologist Karl Kerenyi, gave psychological life to the ancient archetypes, using them to describe the fundamental impulses that lie deeply embedded in the unconscious mind. For him, there were four archetypes, the inner guides that govern our most basic human instincts as hunter, gatherer, lover or mother. Jungian psychologists continue to explore and expand the nature and number of these archetypes to the present day.

Influenced by Jungian theory, spiritual teachings, anthropology, mythology and literature, we have arranged the 24 contemporary male personality profiles found in the western world under a master group of eight archetypes, which together define the dynamics of the masculine self. We believe that our classification offers valuable insights. It's not, of course, a resolution for all the complexities of human nature. But what it reveals about the drives and motivations behind men's behaviour, the different ways in which men reach their potential, and, above all, how different men respond to love makes it a hands-on guide to help you recognize and handle the men you meet. That Hollywood hero may be unreachable. But the men in this book really can be found. They exist. You know them.

Below we list our 24 personality profiles, arranged under their archetypal descriptions, but first an explanation of the terms 'persona' and 'shadow', which you'll find throughout the book. On our journey through life, each of us reveals what we want others to know and like about us. Jung's psychological understanding and interpretation led him to adopt the word 'persona', from the Latin word for an actor's mask, to describe the socially acceptable face with which we protect ourselves, just as the shield and sword protected our soldier ancestors. The 'shadow' is the unrevealed self, kept hidden from others, sometimes so well hidden that even we ourselves forget there is more to us than our persona façade. The shadow personality will naturally play the role of saboteur, causing conflict and making change difficult to achieve.

lover
**philosopher, artist,
obsessive lover, eroticist**

His persona is directed to the pursuit of sensual, romantic, artistic and creative endeavours. His aesthetic consciousness is drawn from his environment. He is influenced by his senses. He feels no separation from the cosmos. His shadow is his self-doubt and angst, his restless irritability, his infantile longings for adoration and his sloth. He is not respectful and has no sense of containment around his sexuality. He may not know how to separate from others.

magician
**performer, bohemian,
fashion luvvie**

His persona has the ability to make his own decisions and take control of his life. He thinks he is invincible. His energy fires progressive thinking. He can create something substantial from raw inspiration. He has transformative power. His shadow is the rebel who insists on his own way. His selfishness will be destructive and his lack of consideration will contaminate his vision. His need for centre stage will alienate him and his high standards and false pride will block opportunities.

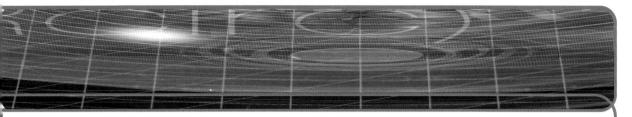

altruist
dr feelgood, zen man

His persona invests in his willingness to put others' welfare before his own. He has accepted his mortality. He generates unconditional positive regard, compassion and enthusiasm. He promotes freedom and generosity of spirit. His shadow is a need to be needed, to fix others' pain. He will co-dependently take on too much responsibility. He will use others to bolster his self-esteem. He will neglect his own personal well-being. He will cross others' personal boundaries.

hero
uniform man, joy junkie, recovering addict, activist

His persona directs him to fight for justice. He has a mission. He is drawn to adventure, chasing the high and taking risks to become the victor. He is a man of admirable exploits and valour. His shadow is his lack of attention to detail. He dances close to the edge of mortality and will ignore warnings. He will not use self-regulation. He will play the blame game.

warrior
entrepreneur, suit, media guy, eco warrior

His persona is motivated by achievement and competition. He cultivates self-sufficiency and champions his primal desires. He is focused on competence and asserts his identity in the world. His shadow is where he hides his guilt. He is aggressive and arrogant. He refuses to unite with others. He will substitute material gain for emotional warmth.

innocent
lad, inheritor, playboy

His persona seeks to gain trust. He can be effective socially and he works hard to establish his place in the world, using a charm that is non-threatening. His naivety is endearing. His shadow is bound by immature behaviour. He will not accept that pain and suffering are part of life. He is insecure and indecisive. He will avoid being accountable for his actions if he makes mistakes.

wanderer
wanderer, cyber man

His persona is his free spirit, which guides him in his journey towards treasure, the gift of his true self. He confronts the unknown in a conscious journey and uses the world to explore experience. He makes the assertion that life is not about suffering but experience. His shadow is rooted in a need to be accountable to no one. He is the lone voyager: he spends too much time in isolation, which may limit his skill in one-to-one interaction.

king
intellectual, dictator

His persona possesses infinite knowledge. He uses his position of strength. He is an upholder of standards and is seen as a leader and an exemplar. He is blessed with wisdom and is often viewed as the wise old man. His shadow is concerned with ways in which he can minimize pain and maximize praise. He can be tyrannical and cruel. He will use unethical methods to seize control. He is blind to his weaknesses and won't hesitate to destroy professional opposition. He detests criticism and can be emotionally frozen if it fits his purpose.

which is the archetype for you?

This quick quiz will help you to find your ideal love match. These seemingly simple questions are designed to analyse your attitude to life and love and to indicate which of the eight contemporary archetypes complement your individual characteristics most favourably.

It's the relationship founded on complementary principles that has the greatest potential to grow and endure through all the cycles of life. To check your answers, see opposite.

1 If you were a pair of shoes what would you be?
a *Strappy, trashy come-and-get-me slingbacks – with handbag to match, naturally.*
b *Your trusty desert boots: they go with everything and they've been everywhere.*
c *Simple, understated low-heeled pumps or unfussy 'street' trainers.*
d *Italian boots, handmade by a craftsman, of the best-quality soft leather.*

2 What is your favourite sex position?
a *Both legs tucked behind your head – a handy move you picked up in your ashtanga yoga class.*
b *Spooning together because it's so intimate, nurturing and gentle.*
c *You don't care so long as you can both watch your-selves in a full-length mirror.*
d *The missionary position: you enjoy being wrapped in your lover's arms, kissing him while you make love.*

3 It's your first weekend away together. What do you do?
a *It's a surprise: he arranges everything from the hotel to the music playing in the background in the restaurant.*
b *He takes you back to the town where he grew up to show you how far he's come in life.*
c *He organizes a weekend white-water rafting in Wales and holds your hand over the rapids.*
d *He locks the two of you away in a secluded country cottage with an open fire and a big, big bed.*

4 Do you have a guru or a role model?
a *Diana, the goddess of hunting: a strong, earthy woman.*
b *Yes. You found him in a cave in Nepal and you use his teachings wherever you are.*
c *You admire Stella McCartney, who combines cutting-edge glamour with a sharp, sassy attitude.*
d *Life is your guru: you look upon everything that happens to you as a learning experience.*

5 What's the most surprising thing about the way you look?
a *Underneath your virginal white dress are layers of red underwear.*
b *You look as good naked as you do dressed – and you look fabulous dressed.*
c *Your fresh, natural, girl-next-door beauty is actually the result of long hours in the salon, the gym and on the sunbed.*
d *You don't know what you look like today: it's weeks since you looked in a mirror.*

6 What's your dream occupation?
a *To go back to university and do a Ph.D. in erotica in the Victorian period.*
b *To work in a Mayfair hair salon – anything to keep your flowing, feminine locks in tip-top condition.*
c *Something worthwhile like researching cures for cancer, or looking after its victims.*
d *To run your own internet travel business and take advantage of all the cheap flights.*

7 What do you love your man to read aloud to you?

a *The love poems of William Butler Yeats or Lord Byron – and by candlelight, of course.*

b *The hottest gossip from the style pages of an independent, underground magazine.*

c *Love letters his grandmother sent to his grand-father during the Second World War.*

d *Passages from the biography of a bold, brilliant man like John F. Kennedy.*

8 What's your favourite drink?

a *Frothy hot chocolate, topped with whipped cream and laced with a delicate Irish liqueur.*

b *A glass of fine, vintage champagne, sipped from a crystal flute.*

c *A hard-to-find energy drink containing guarana that's popular in Brazil.*

d *A delicious, dark, caffeine-free coffee, only available through mail order, with profits going to help plantation workers in Peru.*

9 Do you think a man should make the first move?

a *Yes, always. That's the way it's always been and that's the way it should stay.*

b *No one should make the first move. Your eyes should lock across a crowded room/train/beach and you'll both just know.*

c *No. Let him think he made the first move, but you planned the seduction all along.*

d *No. If you see him and you want him, just go and get him. You always get what you want.*

10 Is infidelity ever acceptable?

a *After marriage, never. Commitment is for life.*

b *Casual sex and meaningless one-night-stands are OK, but emotional involvement with another person is a betrayal.*

c *It depends on who's wooing you: the harder the chase, the more acceptable the infidelity.*

d *There's no such thing as infidelity because you can't ever own another person.*

how did you score?

Each answer corresponds to one of the contemporary archetypes. The archetype with the highest score is the one to which you are best suited. Turn to pages 10–11 for a choice of guys who should turn you on. If two archetypes score equally, there could be more than one type out there for you.

1.
a) Magician
b) Wanderer
c) Innocent
d) Hero

2.
a) Altruist
b) Innocent
c) Magician
d) Hero

3.
a) King
b) Warrior
c) Hero
d) Lover

4.
a) Warrior
b) Wanderer
c) Magician
d) Altruist

5.
a) King
b) Warrior
c) Innocent
d) Wanderer

6.
a) King
b) Lover
c) Altruist
d) Wanderer

7.
a) Lover
b) Magician
c) Innocent
d) King

8.
a) Lover
b) Warrior
c) Hero
d) Altruist

9.
a) Hero
b) Lover
c) Innocent
d) Magician

10.
a) King
b) Wanderer
c) Warrior
d) Altruist

how to use the babes' bible

We believe that by looking at men's specific roles in society, the way they see themselves and the way they are seen by other people, we can gain an insight into why men make certain life choices in work and love. Why, in other words, they behave the way they do.

The 24 personality profiles in this book comprise the basic male types found throughout western society today. As you read, you will discover some personality profiles share traits of behaviour. The Playboy and the Joy Junkie both share the thrill of the chase, but towards different outcomes! Dr Feelgood and the Zen Man are both defined by their concern for the welfare of others. Remember, too, that just as no man is governed by a single archetype, so it's rare to find a man who can be summed up in a single personality profile. Most of the men you meet will be an intriguing web of drives and motivations. It's up to you to identify the exact mix of profiles. But don't forget that your guy is unique.

visual
A window on his world: look carefully and you'll see the symbols that signify who he is.

archetypal description
This is his strong suit, the one that he'll always fall back on. We also include a quick overview of his most identifiable attributes.

persona/shadow
The persona is the revealed and intellectualized psyche. This is information that he wants us to know and believe. The shadow is the concealed and sentimentalized psyche. It's where his true motives live and is said to be responsible for those little slips of the tongue.

aspects of the type
Here we expose his social characteristics: how he conducts himself in public, his attitudes, his will and his intellect.

aspects of the soul
This is where we reveal his deepest and most complex thoughts and feelings. The soul houses his essential nature. Look into his spirit and learn about his inner world. How far along the road of self-discovery has he travelled?

art of love
Clues to his true romantic intentions are outlined for girls with a mission! Decode his dating patterns by looking at his love problem areas and see what you can do to reel him in.

into action/interaction
This is the must-read info. How to catch him, keep him and dump him.

love lesson
Our mission is sister-to-sister wisdom: to give you what you need to love more wisely: to help you choose the right man and protect your heart.

the icons These are your short cut to the key strengths and weaknesses of each personality profile.

availability
Is he free to love? Does he keep his word and will he make you his no.1 priority?

commitment
How well will he meet your wants and desires? Can he make a commitment? And can he live up to it?

sexuality
How well does he perform in and out of the bedroom? Is his concern your pleasure or his? Is he boring or wild? Confident or clumsy?

anger threshold
How mad does he get? Is he a control freak or a bully? A coward or a clean fighter?

social skills
Will your friends like him? Can you take him to meet your mother? Will he protect you and enhance the way other people view you? Or destroy your confidence?

intelligence
He always has to be right, but is he actually Einstein, enigmatic or just exaggerating? And does he know what emotional intelligence means in the real world?

spirituality
Does he stop to help or walk on by? Does he know his mission? Is he on a search for truth? Will he question his existence?

honesty
Does he have the courage to speak the truth, even when it hurts? Is he true to himself? Can you trust him?

love detector
Is he up for love at this time in his life? Is he a romantic or just selfish? Will he follow his head or his heart?

fidelity
Is he an innocent flirt or a dangerous rogue? Can you sleep safe when he's away? Will he be loyal?

playboy

the archetype: The Innocent, seductive wanderer, babe collector, commitment phobic

the persona

how he appears to be

How to spot him – He's the one with eyes on stalks when you walk in. His body language screams, 'I'm the best horn in town'. His wardrobe reinforces the message. He'll be propping up the bar with other likely predators, sharking it.

Dialogue / Verbal – Double entendres and innuendoes, slick in the compliments department. He'll say anything for effect; there's no off-button for this gushing guy.

Chat-line / Pick-up script – 'Do I make you want me, baby?' 'Hey, babe. Lookin' good!' 'I can't take my eyes off you.'

Life course – To carve as many notches on the bedpost as humanly possible. One hundred per cent wolf.

Accessories – His body. His car. His babe cave. His ever-present babe wad.

Day job – Professional playboy, model-agency owner, IT guy who has climbed the ranks of wannabe, mini-celebrity famous for being famous.

Babe history – Lusts them, lures them, licks them and leaves them.

Theme song – 'You're The One That I Want' by Olivia Newton John and John Travolta.

Fantasy – A guest spot on the love yacht, destination Desire Island, where he'll be Robinson Crusoe among a sex-starved cast of naked native women.

the shadow

who he really is

Bad habits – Promises everything but delivers only excuses and little white lies, refuses to turn the babe magnet off in public and boasts about his sex life to your best friend.

What he doesn't say / Secrets and silences – 'I'm a misogynist. Your mother may hate me, but is she sexy? I'm too good for real intimacy – sharing is my thing. Babe, you're in my light.'

Hidden agenda – To pick up and play with; then dump and disappear. To target unassuming women to bolster his fragile ego. To seek fame as a lady-killer.

Philosophical mantra – Travel light.

Accessories – Perma-tan, secret mobile-phone number, second apartment, bottom-drawer G-string collection.

Energy barometer – Parties hard for attention. Morning conversations are out of the question. Over-stimulation brings on orgasm burnout. Has a cigarette after sex. Forgets foreplay and forgets about you.

Relationship future – He'll sacrifice integrity for looks every time. His two-seater sports car is his idea of intimacy. Don't think in the long term until he swaps his self-preoccupation for commitment.

Theme song – 'Sexy Boy' by Air

Sex rating – Good news: always available for sex. Bad news: not always with you.

 10/10 0/10 7/10   5/10

aspects of the type

This type is entertaining, highly sexed and romantic. His passion is fuelled by his longing for the perfect woman. He never gives up the game of entrapment. Often he can be alluring and charming, and he seems genuine to the last. He will take you to a heavenly level of pseudo intimacy, but pseudo is all it is.

He is a self-fulfilling prophecy in relationships: he knows how he's going to initiate and how he's going to finish. This recurring pattern sheds light on his lover-boy complexities. Yes, he gives what appears to be love, but in reality he lives a fantasy that deprives him of true love. His preoccupation is always with getting more (for 'more' read 'sex') and he becomes a slave to his own indulgence as he tries to keep his act together.

A short attention-span is hidden by vast amounts of socializing. You will find him sunglasses, people watching. This guy is a complete wannabe. What other people do or say really does matter to him. The slightest hint of criticism can make him uncomfortable and agitated. He will view it as rejection and, because he refuses to be accountable for his behaviour, he will choose the easy way out and avoid confrontation. And he's not ready to change. He's a heat-seeking missile, looking for a mission. One-night stands are the reward for all that bravado.

Being the centre of attention is great fun for the Playboy. This is his comfort zone. Here he gets his ego boost by feeling wanted, needed and therefore secure. Things go downhill when he loses control. The dynamics change: the high of the pursuit is replaced by a compulsion to wound. As negativity rears its ugly head, what he found adorable he now questions with a cool

He will take you to a heavenly level of pseudo intimacy, but pseudo is all it is.

anywhere but home. He likes the hubbub of noisy, busy places that allow him to expose his outrageously flirtatious behaviour. You might find him casting a curious eye over new outfits in smart stores that cater for the foxy woman. You'll certainly spot him behind a pair of

comeback. As soon as he's got you, he'll be moving on into the departure lounge. If you've fallen for a guy that fits this mould, then wake up. Wonderful as his potential may appear, a leopard never changes his spots. Get your trainers on and start running!

5/10   8/10

aspects of the soul

The Playboy plays. As a confirmed bachelor, he has little concept of long-term sharing. He has never chosen to share as an equal. Somewhere he has learnt to disregard other people to satisfy an egocentric lust for sexual fulfilment. This guy views life as an adventure in hedonism and excess.

He runs around town intent on establishing his masculine identity. In any social gathering it is likely that he will make a statement about himself through his achievements with women. Straightforward virility will be acknowledged and honoured by his peers. They envy his apparent success, elevating him to the status of super stud, and it's validation from other males that feeds his self-esteem. The opinion of women is not so important. His seductive charm tastes sweet yet you are left stranded when he is deceptive, calculating and selfish. The question with this one is, 'Is he deep enough for you?'

His primary goal is to satisfy his fantasy of romantic wickedness. He feels independent and loves to play the wild child who cannot be caught up in the complications and compromises of mature love. By choosing to remain adolescent in this way, he doesn't get bored with life. Yet he is so eager for more of the little intimacy he has experienced that he tries to re-enact each memorable scenario with the latest victim.

He thrives on the idea of infatuation. But he negates any authentic emotional response by reducing every encounter to a matter of sexual attraction. And even this apparently overwhelming urge is not always founded on reality. It is the distortion of reality that satisfies his fantasy. He will cancel any possibility of genuine reaction in an attempt to win more time or less time as he juggles scenarios. To him all is fair in love.

 3/10   2/10

in real life
the local Don Juan

the art of love

A smooth operator: his voice is deep, confident and soft; he is understated and, of course, sexy. He pulls you in with his boyish smiles and come-to-bed eyes. He practised in the mirror when he was a boy. He is the modern-day Peter Pan – eternally young. He is driven by an insatiable appetite for love, or what he substitutes as love. He dreams of the perfect woman, but it is an adolescent dream, based on a fantasy of sexual awakening and perpetuated by the idealization which comes from inexperience. He runs away from growing up, taking responsibility for himself and moving on into the next stage of manhood. In minimizing his opportunities to live as a partner, he limits his growth and remains an 'I' rather than a 'we'. This glitch in his development keeps him immature and constantly seeking diversion from tedium.

He can be viewed as a casualty of the oedipal mother/son relationship. Loving her son too much, the mother finds it difficult to allow him the separation that marks his passage into manhood, and he is doomed to objectify women in his search for the perfect mother replacement. Each woman the Playboy responds to is seen solely in terms of physical beauty as he defines it – image rates much higher than brains or personality – and his entire emotional life is focused intensely upon the latest object of his attention. In every sexual encounter his psyche

relives the adolescent attachment to his mother, but on another level, in an attempt to assert his independence, he takes the cue card to exit from intimacy as he understands it.

Really, this guy is just afraid: his misogyny is both a defence against the 'real thing' (love) and an unresolved attachment to his mother. The dangers of allowing himself to be vulnerable in any equal partnership are too much to bear and he cannot control or conquer this fear. The result: he sabotages the relationships he starts by being unfaithful or at least appearing to be. And so, although he seems independent, he is, in fact, deeply reliant upon a regular hit of romance to make him feel needed. His greatest fear is growing old alone: he may never find the ideal to personify his fantasy of the perfect woman. His depth can be measured by the fact that he does all this knowingly.

The Playboy is a man obsessed with the idea of the chase. He loves to lure women into his trap. His trick is to allow himself to be fascinated by the object of his attentions. His sympathetic charm grants him privileged access to the psychological and emotional state of his prey. But he is an emotional escape artist. He doesn't allow people to get close to him. All of his energy goes into looking relaxed, looking good, having a great time. Don't believe a word he says: put him on your arm but not in your heart.

 2/10 9/10

into action / interaction

the hook

Stand out in the crowd. Look like you're available. He will respond to a come-on so don't be shy. He's played this game before. Be a guilt-free babe and rival his advances. Keep in mind that his flirtatiousness is geared towards arousing sexual feelings; there's no emotional commitment. When you think you've got him, don't relax. Hold him with a feminine helplessness, adding playful disinterest to re-start his libido.

into love

If it's long term, you're in for a rough ride. Prepare yourself for the big come-on to fizzle out. Stand tall in those stilettos and stay in your power. His avoidance of conflict will have you frustrated, especially when he uses humour in an attempt to distract you. Suggest he goes on a male-bonding weekend, where he can find himself! You must be prepared for a little going a long way. Be tender and listen to his every word if he allows you in to his heart.

out of love

When you eventually discover the inevitable – that he's a wolf in sheep's clothing, a boy in a man's suit – leave quietly. Any other way is just not worth the effort. Be realistic about what was real and what was not. Cut your losses and fail fast.

love lesson

Men are fiercely attracted to women who make them feel like sex gods.

joy junkie

the archetype: The Hero, thrill seeker, adrenaline junkie, happy go lucky

the persona

how he appears to be

How to spot him – You'd better be quick – he's never still. The shoes are a giveaway – high-tech sandals or desert boots. Logos define his street cred: cool, contemporary macho. He may even have the muscle to prove it. If in doubt, give him a prod as you pass by.

Dialogue / Verbal – Sports gossip, laced with world-wide weather report and trippy talk. Slope speak, surf chat, skate-board slang – language has been redefined to fit the sport.

Chat-line / Pick-up script – 'You look pretty fit yourself actually.' 'Wanna wax my board?' 'I'll arrange everything – just bring your cagoule.'

Life course – To climb the mountain.

Accessories – Stopwatch, travel agent, boards, skis, boots, fins, blades, sticks, bikes, SPF 30, crash helmet, life insurance, energy drink, huskies.

Day job – Sports-shop salesman, waiter, barman, holiday rep., student, professional competitor, sports instructor, surf/snow bum.

Babe history – He likes to think he's had more women in his bed than there are fleas on an African porcupine.

Theme song – 'Disco Inferno' by The Trammps.

Fantasy – He's just won the lottery and buys himself two tickets to the moon. Blast off in ten seconds: G-force, G-string, G-spot.

the shadow

who he really is

Bad habits – You take second place to his sport fixation. He is impulsive to the point of annoyance. Messy, forgets deodorant, eats quickly and leaves the loo seat up.

What he doesn't say / Secrets and silences – 'I'm scared. Beware of macho leakage. I'm a die-hard chauvinist.'

Hidden agenda – To keep to his own timetable, no restrictions. To break his own record. To be the champion.

Philosophical mantra – I can do it.

Accessories – Condoms, beer bottles, marijuana hothouse, long hair, silly hats, baggy trousers, T-shirt collection, fake driving licence, comics, medals.

Energy barometer – Mind-boggling energy. All that activity gives him a zest for life. He's a handful and he'll expect you to keep up.

Relationship future – Possible, but that's not how he'll see it. He is like a kid in a candy store: he wants to take his pick and enjoy it while it lasts.

Theme song – 'Private Psychedelic Reel' by The Chemical Brothers.

Sex rating – He's not over-sentimental. When it comes down to the nitty gritty, he is in tune with his body but not his brain. What a hunk. Give him a wink as he zips by.

 6/10   2/10   7/10   6/10

aspects of the type

The Joy Junkie is mad about sport, mad about achievement and mad about girls. Life is an adventure. He is on a tight schedule and can be up before dawn if he needs to be. He is energized and carefree. Extroverted and extra-charged. Instinctual. He loves living.

He is hooked on survival and trains hard to achieve his goals. He sets his own targets and is self-motivated. He competes with himself, but not necessarily with anyone else. At amateur level he enjoys what he does because of the thrill it brings. Tobogganing down a mountain faster than sound, his heart pounds, his adrenaline is pumping and his concentration is tight. He is free from fear. This is the high. This is what he has trained himself to do. To reject cowardice and fill himself with faith and courage.

Danger threatens when he pushes himself beyond his limit. This type needs to be cautioned if his ego moves into overdrive. He is obsessed with the notion of challenge and he thinks he's immortal. Risk taking is instinctive to him. He lives for that buzz. It's his divine right. He is proud of how extreme he can be. His dilemma: how can he continue to re-create the excitement he so craves?

Determination, boundless energy and a why-not-you-only-live-once attitude will cause anxiety for anyone not as adventurous. While the rest of the city is sleeping, he is galloping towards his next intense

> ## He is obsessed with the notion of challenge and he thinks he's immortal. He lives for that buzz. It's his divine right.

Socially the Joy Junkie is surrounded by fellow participants. Fearless types hang together. When they mull over a typical day, imaginations run riot with tales of close encounters and narrow escapes. One-upmanship is part of the camaraderie that binds them together. But eagerness to exchange experience is only one of the reasons that make the Joy Junkie part of a team. As a thrill seeker, he is the first to admit his reliance upon it when things go wrong. He trusts it with his life.

encounter. His unconquerable spirit does not recognize the word 'can't'. His mind is racy, though not as fast as his body. He is fun to be around, especially if he avoids being predictable. He has a strong warrior personality, yet his fiercest opponent is himself. The unpredictability of Mother Nature can ruin his mood. On a bad day he is reduced to a sulk. On a good day he'll blow your socks off with his excitement and persistence. He is unruly and wild. Tame him if you dare.

 4/10 5/10

aspects of the soul

When the thrill seeker returns home exhausted from his latest adventure, his enthusiasm is still incandescent. He could glow in the dark. Ever present, ever ready, he is always charged, eager for the next quest. Switching gears does not come easily to this type, but relaxation time is a must. He needs to come back down to earth for the Big Chill.

The Joy Junkie's prayer and meditation is to be always doing. Being is tough. In taking the gift of life for granted, he is young at heart. He is sustained by a faith in the order of the universe, although he doesn't always know if he is taken care of by some higher law. He is a fatalist, a man prepared to take risks and keep an open mind. He won't recognize it but the death wish is strong in him – he simply accepts danger as part of the growing process. This daredevil takes a leap of faith into the zone of the unknown. His spirit is re-energized by the transcendent experiences he has in his sport. He gets the deal, but he doesn't articulate his understanding of fate. This guy has not sold his soul to the devil. Quite the opposite:

he has a profound belief in a power outside himself, a life force. He unites with this life force by way of his physicality. Strong and athletic, he celebrates life in its purest form. He's out there in the world of the living. His soul is a free bird. His playground is a wide open space that he can fly in. He is everywhere and nowhere. He is secure and insecure, young yet wise, silly but serious, all at the same time.

Satisfied only when he's reached his goal, he takes his adventures seriously. Completion and achievement are his reward. These are what bring satisfaction and real happiness. His euphoria spills over, making him great to be around. This hell raiser beams with health. His natural radiance is contagious and his faith in himself is the envy of many. He has lots of spunk. He cites courage as one of the criteria for manhood and he sees his attempts to overcome fear as the testing ground for his masculinity. This is the arena for all his internal questioning. Self-doubt is a state of mind he chooses not to accommodate. In his preoccupation with courage he denies himself the chance to take stock of his life. That, for him, would be risking too much involvement in the mundane world of everyday life.

 4/10 6/10

in real life

the gym fanatic, weekend glider pilot, Antarctic expedition leader, jockey, astronaut trainee, fast driver, jaywalker

the art of love

This guy takes only a minute to fall in love. He's fast on his feet when he sees a cute face with a cheeky grin to match his casual boyishness. All that testosterone and seratonin combine for a powerhouse of sexual energy. Going for gold with women is important to his confidence. The initial attraction is like a red rag to a bull with all those hormones bouncing around. And he *will* charge you!

Love is a component in his life but it's the call of lust that usually grabs his attention. Being so carefree about his love life means that he is a cool dude when it comes to mating and dating. He is so wrapped up in the world of games and adventure. Wooing women is just another high for him. You'll have to out-cool him if he's to bat an eyelash in your direction. But he's a smooth talker if he wants to nail you. He may be prone to exaggeration yet he is a stable character with a fervent love of his sport.

In love you will have to accept taking second place to his adrenaline hit. It gives him the kick he needs for the rest of the day.

You've heard of sports widows? Only the clued-up Joy Junkie will understand that women don't want to be left out of the fun. He is best partnered with a sprightly and sporty babe. The need to compromise will not be so urgent if he can enjoy some of that activity with a partner. He's looking for someone who can hold her own and not be too demanding of his time. The one thing he hates is time-keeping. He abhors imposed schedules, timetables or distant-future plans. He doesn't want to be answerable to anyone. He'll be off and running if you try to fence him in. He's having the time of his life and he's not able to take things seriously.

If you fit the glass slipper, his heart will open to love. But this type is not as straightforward as he seems. He'll be quite prickly about where his heart lies. His wild-child attitude can be immature and selfish, and these are traits that may block his romantic happiness. It's a shame he is so darn gorgeous – what with his vitality and determination. This dude is hip, happy and hot to trot.

 4/10   8/10

into action / interaction

the hook

Dress down and get down on it for this guy. He wants to see you in action. Burn, baby, burn. He likes a bit of sweat and grime in his extra-curricular activities. He loves to feel alive so show him that you are! Flirting must be done with a laidback I-don't-really-care attitude. This will snatch him, no problemo. His charisma, joy and sheer sexuality steer him towards the nearest sexy babe. He loves a challenge so act irreverent.

into love

He absolutely adores to eat, sleep and breathe. Make sure it's with you. Big tip: in the honeymoon phase, a mere lunar cycle for this guy, never ever, ever whine. He needs to know the benefits of being in a relationship with you. Put boundaries in place when it comes to time and fidelity. Get involved and feel the exhilaration of riding the crest of this guy's wave. Keep your balance at all times. Have courage.

out of love

If you get fed up with sand in the sheets, dirty laundry and never going out on a romantic date, quit over the phone. You won't outpace him face to face.

love lesson

This life is not a rehearsal. Claim your seat on the roller coaster.

entrepreneur

the archetype: The Warrior, adventurous achiever, believer, success machine

the persona

how he appears to be

How to spot him – He is cool and slick and, because he is comfortable with who he is, he can hold any audience. Fine wines and cigars were his props before they were anyone else's.

Dialogue / Verbal – User-friendly. A good listener, he makes you feel at ease: wants to know your life story without giving away his. Global and anecdotal, boisterous but not brash, witty when he's pressed to impress.

Chat-line / Pick-up script – 'Hi, let me introduce myself.' 'Fancy a day at the races?' 'Didn't I see you in Cap Ferrat last week?'

Life course – To climb the ladder of success through his own efforts. To meet his destiny.

Accessories – Chauffeur, housekeeper, Cordon Bleu chef, occasional personal trainer, platinum cards, so *nouveau riche* friends, pilot licence, art collection, wine cellar, antique car.

Day job – Property developer, restaurateur, sandwich and sushi chain owner, coffee-company franchiser, financial investor, web-site inventor.

Babe history – In the beginning there was sweet-thing, followed by babe-brain, but it's trophy wife that gets her claws in.

Theme Song – 'Material Girl' by Madonna.

Fantasy – Voted top of the Fortune 500 list, he picks and chooses from ensuing fan mail.

the shadow

who he really is

Bad habits – Work comes first; you come second. Over-committed, unscrupulous, greedy as opposed to green. Blinded by materialism, he buys his way out of problems. Take-over tactics in business and in bed. Confidence turns to conceit.

What he doesn't say / Secrets and silences – 'Without my money I'm nothing.'

Hidden agenda – To jettison anything that blocks his highway to the high life. To be the object of social chitchat.

Philosophical mantra – Nothing is more attractive than confidence.

Accessories – Pre-nuptial agreement, fast-food take-away habit, insomniac aids.

Energy barometer – He doesn't know when to stop and may be burnt out; stuck in top gear when rivalling the new kids on the block.

Relationship future – Great providers are potentially great nest builders, but make sure his days of road-testing the competition are really over.

Theme song – 'Stairway to Heaven' by Led Zeppelin.

Sex rating – A well-practised man of this type will always deliver. Experience is the greatest teacher. The promise of divine delights will keep you on your toes.

 2/10   6/10   6/10   7/10

aspects of the type

Greatness and the journey of the hero inspire him. To realize his dream, he'll do whatever it takes. He sees self-discipline and drive as the key components for a winning script. His secret weapon is an unswerving ability to stay focused. From conception to completion, each stage of a project is sacred. It literally is 'his baby'.

In many ways this type yearns to make a difference, to leave his mark on the world. Individuality is the name of his game, although he seems to seek self-generated social status. Uninhibited by stories of failure, the Entrepreneur relies on an inner reservoir of optimism and

He has the single-mindedness and courage to break free from the confines of his existence and become master of his own destiny. Transformation allows him to embrace new perspectives. His ability to take control of his life is central to his development and success. But beware: as he realizes his dreams, he may become suspicious of newcomers' motives in befriending him. People, he is convinced, want to take from him. It becomes difficult for him to ask for emotional support in a crisis. He knows the saying, 'If you don't have a plan for your life, someone else does.'

Defeat is apparently a word that has no place in his vocabulary.

sound judgment. Experience has taught him that there is a place for risk-taking.

He is prepared to innovate, harnessing the pace of economic and social change as he pursues business opportunities in the quickest and most advantageous way. He makes his fortune by persuading others that their interests lie alongside his own. He finds fulfilment by contributing to his friends and family, his business and the wider community.

Defeat is apparently a word that has no place in his vocabulary. He is driven to accept new challenges: life is a daring adventure or nothing. In his psyche, however, it's a completely different story. He has a great fear of failure, of losing everything he has gained. His worst-case scenario would be to wake and find that he has nothing – possession connects with his self-worth and he would feel literally worthless.

6/10   6/10

aspects of the soul

This man craves security. Why else would he be motivated to pursue money and status? He's a winner and he won't stop till he drops. But holding on to first prize is where the stress creeps in.

He realizes that life is a wheel of fortune with its highs and its lows. Events have not always worked in his favour. Maybe he was the boy who started the lemonade stand down by the shore and worked long hours in all weather. He has had to face real disappointment since then. But his determination and commitment are impressive and helped him to deal with all the challenges along the way. His achievement is testament that he is able to survive the hardships of life, but can he continue to work the trick as the wheel turns again?

Curiosity is instinctive to the Entrepreneur. This is what drives him with wide-eyed excitement to shape his life to accommodate the limitless possibilities that come his way. Courage fuels this man's determination: he searches his soul for strength, blocks out despondency and focuses on accomplishment. Being Mr Confidence is what gives him the ability to take the leap of faith each day. Having a passion for his interests is also vital, and so is the capacity for hard work.

The Entrepreneur can be a very approachable character: he involves himself directly in every enterprise. Being around him is compelling because his can-do attitude instills self-esteem in others and opens the door to experimentation where the sky's the limit.

 4/10   6/10

in real life

the one-man band, door-to-door salesman, fast-food retailer, franchisee, import—export guy

the art of love

This guy is turbo-charged with a real zest for life. He loves to get the best out of everything. He can turn a negative into a positive any time he wants. Emotionally, he operates on two levels: there's his childlike sense of wonderment and the adult aggression he needs to make things happen. His bullishness will appear hard-headed to those that challenge him but the flip side is his loyalty.

He is consistently focused and this prevents him from realizing his goals in love. Caught up in his world of acquisition and security, he sees his success as a benchmark for others to live up to. His constant need for quick results works against him in his emotional life, and he is frequently deaf to his inner voice as he allows himself little time for reflection.

His relentless drive to pursue more money, more status, may cover an emotional bankruptcy. The whirlwind of activity keeps his heart closed. He is a doer rather than a feeler. He needs to learn how to stop and allow his feelings to surface. This is profoundly frightening for the Entrepreneur: in striving to prove himself to the outside world, he disconnects from people who simply need his love and time. He tells himself the next deal will be the one to make him contented, excusing himself as he avoids becoming deeply involved with any partner.

Equating emotional strategies with business structures, he is fearful of being double-crossed. Because love is unpredictable, he plays it safe, finding total commitment difficult. His self-protectiveness and jealousy can contaminate any potential for trust. Not recognizing the freedom that comes from sincerity, the Entrepreneur may miss out on what is being offered to him.

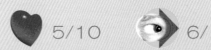 5/10   6/10

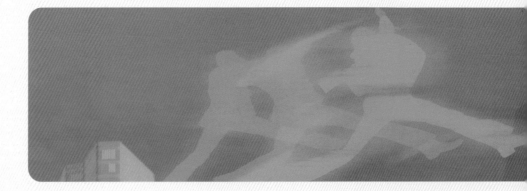

into action / interaction

the hook

This guy is looking for someone he can trust. Build a friendship and win his heart. Ace small talk will help him relax in your company. Make him believe that he can find harmony with you. He's got to know that you need him: signs of well-placed affection will warm his heart. Reassure him by being true to your word.

into love

Be honest about your intentions. He admires a woman who knows how to honour her own heart and has a clear focus on her own life within a relationship. He is attracted to people who strive for achievement and success; his new worlds were discovered through competitiveness. If this is the guy for you, tempt him out of his insecurities. Make it possible for him to realize his fear of failure. Be expansive in every way with him.

If you make it to high-maintenance babe, just remember the achiever treadmill: it's up to you to take his attention away from tomorrow and ground him in the here and now. Synergy through teamwork will seal the deal and keep you together.

out of love

Distance yourself by slowly withdrawing from him. This guy will automatically feel betrayed. He will question your reasons for wanting to move out of the relationship so try to instigate a realistic discourse in which you can assure him of your good intent and counterbalance his feeling of forfeit. He will learn the value of taking risks in love.

love lesson
Honour your own aspirations as well as his.

suit

the archetype: The Warrior, corporate clone, number cruncher, deal clincher

the persona

how he appears to be

How to spot him – In grey, in black, in pinstripes, in fresh neckband. Ready for the eight o'clock meeting, suited and booted, or in the commuter nightmare of shaven whiskers and short back and sides.

Dialogue / Verbal – A fast talker, he gets to the point quickly. Well-mannered with a streamlined accent, but one-to-one makes him hot under the collar.

Chat-line / Pick-up script – 'Would you like to have dinner with me?'

Life course – To be well heeled sooner rather than later.

Accessories – Business cards, electronic diary, duty-free ties, paperback by male thriller writer, downsized expense account, gym bag with squash racket, sad dog at home alone.

Day job – Banker, accountant, insurance broker, legal eagle, sales manager, consultant, chairman, corporate executive officer.

Babe history – Friday night and it's all right. Singles scene is the meat rack: babes on sticks. By Sunday brunch at the pub, she could be a bloody Mary.

Theme song – 'Money, Money, Money' by Abba.

Fantasy – Buy the company, seduce the chairman's daughter, fill a private jet with bimbos and escape the humdrum.

the shadow

who he really is

Bad habits – Anal retentive. Refuses to question his own limitations, doesn't crack good jokes, can't handle his drugs and forgets his niece's birthday.

What he doesn't say / Secrets and silences – 'If we go to my parents at the weekend, could you wear a dress? I'm under pressure.'

Hidden agenda – To play it safe and avoid making waves. To be seen as the wonder boy. To get a lot from a little. To cover up his mistakes.

Philosophical mantra – Hard-earned happiness is doubly savoured.

Accessories – Hair transplant, alarm clock, deodorant and breath freshener, money plant, *Financial Times*, erotic web sites accessed on his PC at work.

Energy barometer – Level at pre-dinner drinks, high at dinner, plummeting to a low by the time you are ready to go home. He's dreaming of duvet therapy with or without you – he's past caring – but he'll have a stab. Just to see the outcome.

Relationship future – Nuclear family: 1.8 children, the seven-year itch.

Theme song – 'Boys Don't Cry' by The Cure.

Sex Rating – Sex on Fridays if he's single, Sundays if he's married. The rest of the week depends on alcohol points.

 5/10   7/10   4/10   8/10

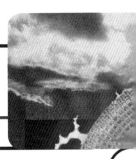

aspects of the type

The Suit is smart. He follows in the footsteps of the bowler-hat brigade, the Suit Dinosaurs of days gone by when one's word was one's bond. Whether he is a product of the education system – school, then university – or a graduate of the school of life, he has been enticed into the big boys' world of spondoolicks. He wants the guarantee of a future, the rewards of a fast-changing business world and maybe a doorway to job heaven. But has he got the strength, the drive? Can he handle the fast pace of the floor? Can he eat grit? The sad news is that not many of them make it to boardroom level, and then only if they can prove their worth to the firm.

guidance and corporate coaching on tap: conflict-resolution programmes and communication-skills seminars are all available. But always the emphasis is on reaching targets, and success is celebrated only in monetary terms. Any sense of achievement is a purely by-product, the desire for recognition is callously manipulated and company relationships play no real part in company monitoring. The result? Toxic egos run riot.

This type works hard. He puts the hours in. It's tough in a predominantly male environment with its lack of compassion and trust. You never can tell who the bad guys are. Their faces all look the same. The daily fight to survive reinforces his masculine

The daily fight to survive reinforces his masculine energies.

The man is struggling to maintain his identity in a workplace that gives him both the chance to shine and the occasion to be dehumanized if he lets the internal politics of the job get to him. This world is a strain on him personally and professionally because of the demand to deliver results. It's a threatening environment, where he has to work alone but is answerable to a team. Time pressure may reduce contact with the boss to a stream of e-mails designed to head off a dressing-down. And can you blame him? Sure, he has management

energies, and this is why he remains focused on competence and achievement. If he displays incompetence, he could get hurt. If he is fierce, he can win. A competitive edge is essential in this man's world. So are curtness and abruptness but they only intensify the struggle for self-worth. Ironically this guy probably has a predetermined role. His profile, his trajectory, has been recorded since the first interview. He is at the mercy of the powers that be. Company hierarchy usually wins.

 7/10   4/10

aspects of the soul

A spiritual approach to life in the financial market is unlikely and counter-productive. Money is God and the US economic gurus the inspiration. This type lives in a world of conflict. There is little time for anything other than the pursuit of winning. He is obsessed with achievement. He places no importance on looking inwards. The competitive streak drives him. The end-of-year bonus is his reward for performance.

He values obedience and conformity to the status quo. What's left of the old-boy network provides close ties with colleagues and adds to his sense of security. But his peer group represents a threat and enforces the need for killer tactics – you just never know who's going to stab you in the back. A crucial aspect of his inner world is his desire to prove himself to his superiors. He entered the industry fresh faced and enthusiastic. Soon his defences are established well enough for him to avoid losing face. This type exudes self-control. Really he is accessing his warrior defences to slay the dragons and anything else that interferes with his master plan. He is insecure and afraid that he will go unrecognized if he does not deliver.

Slowly he is corrupted: it's the only way to survive in this environment. True human interaction is replaced with stand-over tactics. The fine line between assertion and aggression is often crossed. In this battlefield of corporate psychopaths no courtesy is afforded to other people's needs or requirements. Interpersonal relationships have little decorum, irrespective of rank, and higher status wins hands down. The main motivation is greed. The pay-off is all-consuming superiority.

Finally, man becomes monster. Human compassion is extinct, fairness goes out the window and he would sell what's left of his soul to clinch the deal. He enjoys the fruits of his working life. His triumphant attitude speaks volumes. He sees himself as victorious in his fight for survival. He is keenly aware that should he lose his golden-boy sparkle he will be left behind, simply sidelined, replaced and forgotten. Under no circumstances can he afford to be seen as a soft touch. His view of the world is consumed by cynicism. Remorse just doesn't register. If it did, he'd be scribbling a letter of resignation.

 2/10   3/10

in real life
the B.Sc. (Hons.) graduate, cynical middle-aged insurance broker, barrow boy turned trader, clever estate agent, guy they had to let go on the rebound.

the art of love

The pleasure bond for this type is strongly situated in the physical. He has a hang-up about appearance (his and hers) and the status attached to it. He is big on fantasies. He views love as short term, an opportunity to exploit as many partners as possible. The Suit's male ego is driven by the accumulation of power. He is under pressure with a limited career span: he'll burn out faster here than in any other workplace.

This guy only gets serious when he tires of the chase and decides that he wants children. He is on the lookout for a partner who is willing to slip into his lifestyle and will be acceptable on a social level but he is very aware that there is no hurry. What he has to offer is stability and shelter in a world of ever-changing gender roles. If you're tempted, be warned: the Suit will shape the family unit in accordance with his own ideals, strengths and weaknesses. His emphasis on discipline and financial gain are values that he will look for and foster in a suitable partner.

Once this guy has decided to take a relationship seriously, he will triumph over his apparent emotional alienation and allow himself to communicate at a deeper level. However, at times the workplace ethic of dog-eat-dog spills over into his personal life. The Suit's self-esteem intensifies if success involves a struggle. He is a misguided warrior because he has been taken in by a materialistic culture and lost sight of who he is. To sustain the satisfaction of gaining more status, more power, more money, he indulges in savage organizational politics. In love he soothes himself in the knowledge that he has the external requirements to lure the women of his choice.

At the beginning of the relationship he is most available and most connected to his fantasies. Unfortunately a seam of chauvinism reinforces the pressure he puts on his partner to earn him points and praise from his peers and superiors. Crucial to any relationship with a Suit is reciprocity. He demands that she look gorgeous in front of his colleagues and friends; in return, she gets to be shown off.

 4/10   8/10

into action / interaction

the hook

Respond to any come-ons by being sweet and sincere. He likes the well-groomed look. Young and fresh gains Brownie points and keeps you in his little black book. If you want to hold the spotlight, listen to this first-hand anecdote. A Suit once called his girlfriend to request that she 'wear a skirt short enough to show the gap between her thighs'. Get shopping.

into love

He needs to realize his potential for enjoying life without the fight. Introduce him to the world beyond work. Let him rest when he comes home to you and don't bombard him until he has unwound. Changing his old-school attitude towards 'coupledom' will be hardgoing but you will both benefit when the lines of communication are opened up. Make him feel that he has nothing to prove when he is with you.

out of love

If he is unable to give you heart space, don't give up too easily. Suggest a respite from the relationship. Re-evaluate your situation. If you want out because you don't feel he is committed enough, then ask him for commitment. If he says he is not ready, believe him and keep kissing those frogs!

love lesson

You gain more by finding a rich seam and digging deep than by flitting from one shallow mine to another.

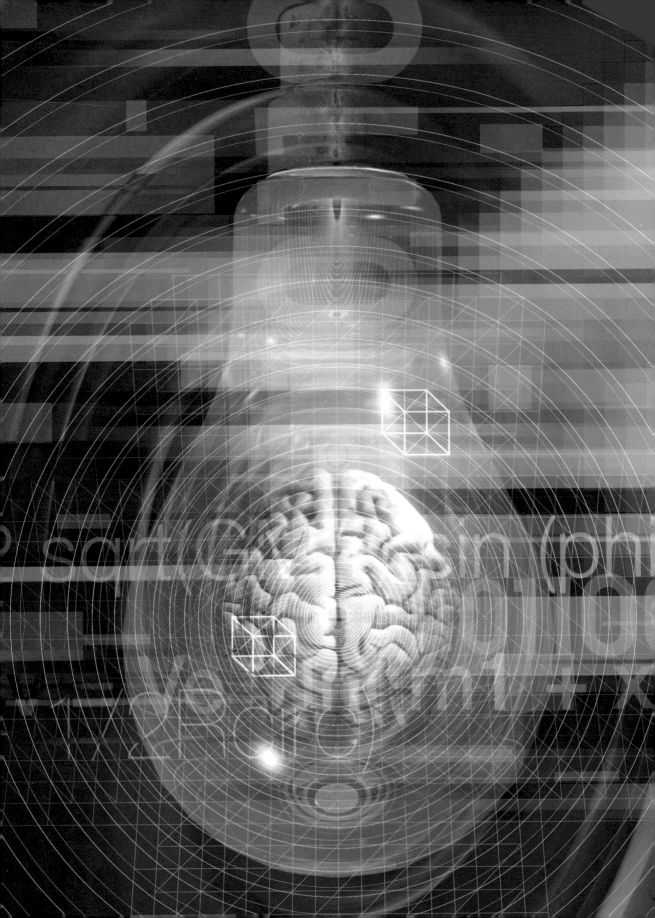

intellectual

the archetype: The King, knowledge generator, cerebral gymnast, think tank

the persona

how he appears to be

How to spot him – Locked in a stalemate at the chess tournament or in the hot-seat at a MENSA convention. Check for corduroy or velvet, and odd socks. The scarf is definitive when it's chilly.

Dialogue / Verbal – Well researched. Cryptic at first, building up to information overload. He speaks with clarity, but will send your head into a spin with his theories, if invited.

Chat-line / Pick-up script – 'Are you a student of mine?' 'You're not just a pretty face, are you?'

Life course – To draw his own conclusions. To pioneer the field.

Accessories – Study, dusty *objets trouvés*, well-worn book bag, personalized filing system, database, slide projector, multiple library cards, periodical subscriptions, bow tie.

Day job – Professor, lecturer, high-flying civil servant.

Babe history – The last one left because he wouldn't marry her. Doe-eyed women are always in with a chance.

Theme song – 'Air On a G String' (from Orchestral Suite no.3) by J.S. Bach.

Fantasy – A dangerous liaison: he's seduced by a quiz-show hostess on live TV. His finger's on the buzzer and all the answers are correct. Clever boy.

the shadow

who he really is

Bad habits – Laughs out loud when he thinks what you're saying is ludicrous. Debit in the romance column and incredibly vague – misplaces house keys, bicycle and pets. Is messy, buries his head in the newspaper and times himself doing the crossword.

What he doesn't say / Secrets and silences – 'I'm absorbed by my work. I won't be home in time for dinner. I don't have good hand–eye co-ordination. I find the opposite sex illogical.'

Hidden agenda – To win the Nobel Prize.

Philosophical mantra – I think, therefore I am.

Accessories – Stressed research assistant, stuffed animals in the bedroom, potted plants, receding hair line, one piece of extraordinary jewellery, abacus, politically correct attitude.

Energy barometer – Always busy. He scuttles here, he scuttles there, spreading himself thin and taking on work like it's going out of fashion.

Relationship future – Looking for a well-educated woman who wears suspenders.

Theme song – 'Why Does My Heart Feel So Bad?' by Moby.

Sex rating – He'll beguile you with his authoritative embrace. All work and no play means that you'll have to remind him of basic biology, but he's a fast learner.

 6/10 7/10 5/10 4/10

aspects of the type

An Intellectual is big in the brain-cells department. And, as the saying goes, size counts! He is not a philosophical type necessarily. His trump card is his constant curiosity. He loves to be fascinated. Information – facts, data, statistics, theories – is his oxygen. Without it who would he be? His personality revolves around his need to marshal knowledge to support logical argument. Reason is his reason for being, and his passion is to solve problems and to prove or disprove the opinions of others. Semantics thrill him to bits.

He will always rise to the occasion if challenged intellectually. He adores a good argument and gets his jollies by rattling other people's cages. The guy is super alert, incisive and uses logic to run circles around anyone who takes him on. He will respect those who know conversation that he deems worthy of his participation. His head tilted to one side with a furrowed brow, he'll be looking downwards, oblivious of the crowd. It is not easy for him to sustain eye contact if he is analysing a concept. The ignition key has been turned and his mind is elsewhere already.

This type will travel effortlessly through the barriers of class. An intellectual snob he might be, but he is not a snob in the social sense. He has a tendency to bee-line for brain power and he is happy to enjoy brilliant minds wherever he finds them. It's for this reason that

His trump card is his constant curiosity.

what they are talking about and has no time for pseudo-intellectuals or navel gazers. Female logic certainly baffles him: he finds it annoying yet oh so endearing ... captivating even. But he has little patience with ignorance and no patience with fools, dismissing them bluntly without ceremony. And, annoying as this will be, he'll be convinced that he's right.

Socially, he loves to be part of a set that appreciates his brilliance. He enjoys highbrow discussion, either one to one or with a group of trusted friends or colleagues. It's easy to spot an Intellectual at a social event. He'll look fascinating if he's deeply immersed in Intellectual types often pair up with unusual people.

The quirky aspect to his personality is the way he relates to those outside his circle. Usually an introverted type, he may at first be seen as reserved or indifferent, but this is because he is not the kind to try to impress himself on those who are not asking. Superficiality is not his bag. On the other hand he may be just watching and waiting for the right moment to join (and win) the argument. This is a guy whose idea of the perfect world includes him always having the last word.

 10/10   3/10

aspects of the soul

The Intellectual's all-time favourite topic is the theory of creation. The questions of how the universe began and how it will end are constantly intriguing for this type. To talk about his soul is not so easy. Outside the framework of scientific theory he will struggle to find an explanation of how and why he exists. To debate the issues concerning the soul's existence he demands concrete evidence – evidence that he can measure, analyse and organize. To arrive at a satisfactory answer he must be able to prove through logical argument. His emphasis on reason and knowledge leads him to minimize the importance of anything that cannot be tested within his frame of reference.

But the soul is not found through intellect, through rational experience. It derives meaning and value directly from life experience. The notion of an existence that is not entirely quantifiable is what confuses the Intellectual. Understanding who he is at a deep and personal level becomes hazardous for him. A brilliant mind cannot lead him to wisdom.

Spiritual matters are inextricably linked to a person's feelings, emotions and actions, and this type finds it less easy to communicate with himself and the expressive part of his psyche. The deciphering of his soul is blocked by his relatively low emotional intelligence, the accumulation of interactive skills which play various roles in personal relationships.

This guy strives to cope with what he perceives as a critical world by constructing a perfect outer life. He may be aware that his preoccupation with perfection drives him away from other people, but success is important to him. It's not his soul that he shows to outsiders after all; it's his intellectual achievement. He sets himself very high standards which he cannot always attain, and he is anguished when he feels that he has not fulfilled his objectives. This is why so many Intellectual types are workaholics.

By not allowing himself the chance to experience the ebb and flow of a rich emotional life, the Intellectual denies the opportunity to connect with his spirit at its deepest levels. Instead he imitates the perfection of a higher being through his perfectionist personality and this becomes his 'sense of soul'.

 4/10    6/10

in real life
the inventor in the garden shed, prodigy, mature student, rocket scientist, pub mathematician, puzzle master

the art of love

The Intellectual in love is time warped in shy-schoolboy behaviour. Flirting is foreign to him, and, although there's no doubt that he is a man with a beating heart, if you have any hope that he will carry you upstairs and throw you on the bed on the first date, forget it!

This is a type who likes to take his time when he joins the dance of love. Dealing with an Intellectual guy in love is like betting on the tortoise on the racetrack. He's slow but, given the chance, he'll overtake the hare. He dislikes risk. He will want to evaluate and judge the stages of love. But he will respond to seduction if the time is right. What will really titillate him is if you have the confidence to switch roles: let him play pupil while you play teacher.

He is excited by any intellectual challenge and will search for a lover who has wit coupled with brains. Academic achievement will more than likely be important to him and he values the thirst for knowledge in his partner. What's inside is more important than what's outside.

Alas, logic will not always compensate for his lack of awareness in emotional matters. Bear in mind that the main reason for failure with an Intellectual type is his strong impulse to be competitive. Long-term happiness will only be achieved if he finds a woman to satisfy his analytical requirements, one with whom he can also build a dialogue. Having a partner he can talk to will satisfy him enormously so he is best suited to a conscientious woman who can appreciate and support his need to be mentally stimulated. Paradoxically he prefers the ups and downs of sparky, spontaneous meetings of minds because this keeps challenge alive.

When faced with dilemmas of the heart, the Intellectual will not be as in tune with the needs of his partner as you would hope. His resistance to solving simple emotional problems comes from his particular viewpoint: he will consider what should be done, and not what needs to be done. And he will challenge his partner to mirror his sense of responsibility and commitment. His black-or-white approach to everything can mean that it's all or nothing with this one.

The Intellectual in love may be conservative. He finds it an effort to share intimacies because he is not in tune with his feelings. He is bashful and hesitates before revealing his wish list. But thinking about the mysteries of love will intrigue him. His idiosyncrasies are sure to put a smile on your face and, just as the universe still holds many mysteries, so too has the Intellectual in love.

♥ 6/10   5/10

into action / interaction

the hook

Total seduction is the best way to clear away those cobwebs! Undress him on the first date. Surprise him again by dropping in topics of conversation that you know will whet his appetite for romance. Win his affections by having the confidence to have your own convictions. Above all, don't be afraid to disagree with him if you know you are right.

into love

Don't come across as too gregarious: this will scare him off big time. Your self-improvement goals and dependability will stop him worrying. To keep the interest alive be the thinking man's crumpet, sparking the intellectual connection between you by digging into his mind.

Create an outlet to discuss problems openly instead of internalizing them. This will make or break the relationship – either way, it will be much easier to get to know him. The more you introduce him to alternative ways of encountering life, the more he will ease into your arms.

out of love

He may drive you to distraction by needing to win the argument all the time. If power struggles crop up, try to stand back from them. If this fails and you want out, don't debate the issue or you'll never leave. He will cut off from you emotionally to self-protect. Let him do this without taking it to heart.

love lesson

Work on getting some letters after your name. Keep the dialogue of love flowing by initiating intellectual pastimes of the heart. Write a love letter or two ...

eroticist

the archetype: The Lover, trickster, breaker of sexual taboos, creates his own moral universe

the persona

how he appears to be

How to spot him – His body language is overt: he knows who he is, what he's about and what he wants.

Dialogue / Verbal – If he gets the signal, small talk turns to sexual innuendo, pronto!

Chat-line / Pick-up script – 'Has anyone ever told you that you have come-to-bed eyes?' 'We both think you're ravishing.'

Life course – To experiment with out-of-the-ordinary sexual acts.

Accessories – Mood lighting, well-stocked bar, sexy cigarette lighter, phallic cacti, roman candles, oysters, oversized bed, two-way mirrors, erotic art, books, films and tapes, jacuzzi, little black book.

Day job – Porn star, nude photographer, sexual 'healer', amateur-video producer, pimp, sex-club owner, S & M supplier, hedonism party organizer.

Babe history – He's had a great time experimenting, exploring and exciting. Straight babes ran a mile and the kinky ones hung around to smile.

Theme song – 'If You Want My Love' by Jennifer Lopez.

Fantasy – To be the biggest and the best, taking endless pleasure and the right measure of pain with an inexhaustible supply of fetishistic props and attire.

the shadow

who he really is

Bad habits – Unexplained absences. Never answers questions about his past, locks the bathroom door, phones 0800 numbers, propositions your girlfriend, looks over your shoulder at parties and borrows your underwear. He can be a day-time dominatrix.

What he doesn't say / Secrets and silences – 'I'm weirder than you thought. I want to share you. I swing both ways. I'm a quick-change artist. I can see your nipples.'

Hidden agenda – To be an agent provocateur.

Philosophical mantra – I'm a connoisseur of sex.

Accessories – High-magnification binoculars, handcuffs, bondage equipment, dog collar, whip, leather boots, blindfold, genital jewellery, sex toys, massage oils, collection of masks, password.

Energy barometer – Off-the-dial sexual energy: highly stimulated by possibilities of what might be and always ready to respond.

Relationship future – Ideally, he wants his sexual 'twin', but in the meantime he'd rather be a loner. It's less complicated.

Theme song – 'Sexual Healing' by Marvin Gaye.

Sex rating – Quickly aroused, if you know what turns him on. He'll surprise you with his infinite variety of party tricks.

 9/10 3/10 8/10 8/10

aspects of the type

The Eroticist is a classic example of one extreme of the human psyche. He pursues perhaps the oldest of our pleasures – sexual gratification. He departs from what is considered the norm in sexual behaviour, and in that sense he is different. But the word is not used in any judgmental sense. Unlike the Playboy, who is motivated by the chase, the Eroticist is interested in the act. This sexpert likes to explore and live out his sexual fantasies, giving and receiving in mutual acts of pleasure. Desires do not cause him conflict because of his ability to act upon them.

He will look and act like the average man around town, but he won't draw unnecessary attention to himself. He is the kind of guy that watches the action from the edge of the crowd. You can pick him out by observing him observing you. He doesn't miss a thing. He is sociable but reserved, gleaning any reference that could initiate contact. As an open-minded individual, he knows how to make people feel at ease. The nature of his sexuality means that he can reveal the quirkier side of himself only if he establishes trust, and his moral code dictates that he should go only where he is wanted. He must never force another to join his world.

He may feel maligned by society's often phobic opinions on sexuality. His defence is withdrawal. He will protect his private space so that he can keep a distance from the outside world if he needs to. Safe distance equates to protection from unwanted exposure. Any confidential exchange is inevitably highly charged. It is the guarantee of shared secrecy that is his primary reassurance.

He has a voracious appetite for all kinds of visual information, using it to feed his active fantasy life. His appreciation of erotica spills into the world of aesthetics. He is titillated by painting, sculpture, nude photography and film noir, and he escapes from day-to-day life into the world of his imagination to maintain a high level of excitement.

You can pick him out by observing him observing you.

5/10   4/10

aspects of the soul

This man will flirt with danger to reach a sexual high. He has discovered, to his delight, an outlet for his imaginative game-playing, a place where he can be accepted and appreciated. He mingles with a wide community of sexual purveyors: people who meet regularly to experience a sexual psycho-drama that embraces the extremes of sado-masochism, bondage, auto-erotic sex, fetishism, orgy, role playing and humiliation. He is happy in the freedom to widen his sexual frontiers and sees no reason why sexuality cannot be as explorative as other areas in life.

The notion of a secret life, a life out of the ordinary, appeals to him. He may believe that when feelings become painful they should be let go. Certainly his lifestyle enables him to compartmentalize his emotional life and his sexuality. This type is highly ritualistic and a perfectionist, like the men who choose to return to the same prostitute in the same room at the same time. He enjoys being surrounded by the mysterious paraphernalia of sexual personification. Whatever the ritual, he sets it up to keep total control at all times.

He is a compulsive type who allows for a limited range of emotions in the sexual act. He may shout, he may laugh, he may scream, but this is all part of the process of physical satisfaction. He experiences orgasm in its most basic, biological state. The moment of genital release is the point at which he bonds with his partner. Unless he is in a committed relationship, it will be his only point of contact with the other person. If he is a voyeur, he will allow his emotions to emerge only in private.

When he retreats from his escapades, his soul longs to be at peace. Because he is so detached from other people, he finds great release in his fantasy life. His escapist soul is cushioned by strong visualization. His aesthetics are surreal and personal. He edits reality to make sense of his world and uses euphoric recall to relive sublime moments.

 3/10   2/10

in real life

the peeping Tom, foot fancier, over-enthusiastic sex-shop salesman, cross dresser, spanker

the art of love

The Eroticist is not a great communicator and any relationship depends on disclosure. Self-protection is always his first line of defence. He recoils from spontaneity, and his need for predictability may have led him to isolation as an observer, an outsider. Emotional cut-off and spiritual non-attachment have combined. For this guy, sexual behaviour is the preferred way to interact with a partner. Being close in a non-verbal way requires very little contact to sustain a relationship.

He may for years have been a loner, participating in anonymous sex. Nameless faces and places are convenient because privacy is essential: he can live out his secret sexual fantasies without being judged. He can delay or withhold emotion. Or he may have been involved with a regular group. If so, he is more likely to feel secure, and group dynamics allow for a whole host of enticing experiments, including the polarities of dominator and dominated.

If love is to become possible, the Eroticist needs to share with a partner who has the same sexual energy. He can be a hot number, confident in his display of non-verbal sexual communication – sexy, outrageous and instinctive. When he shares his sexual being with another, he shares what is sacred to him. If you both indulge the taboo, a strong sense of intimacy will be forged because you will have found someone to accept your sexual preferences and to allow your need for privacy. Rejection ceases to be an issue.

If he commits to you, life could become hair-raising, eye-popping, spine-tingling and wild. Intense encounters can be brief but if he is in love they will be much more meaningful. You will exchange more confidences than other lovers. There is a good chance that if this guy is ready for love he will also become your confidant and your agent provocateur.

3/10   9/10

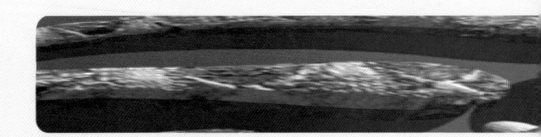

into action / interaction

the hook

Undress him with your eyes. Wiggle your toes and tighten your belt. Whisper, 'I'm just going to slip into something more comfortable.' Mirror all his actions. When he smiles, you smile. When he reaches out to touch you, reach out to touch him. Maintain contact. Make it intense. Up the volume, dim the lights and remove an item of clothing. But not too soon.

into love

Keep him full of desire and longing. He loves to be in this state. He dislikes competitive or confrontational situations so save any power struggles for bedtime fantasy. Indulge your passion for sensuality. It may take time to come to terms with a one-on-one setup. You will both need to feel uninhibited and understood. Banish wistful longings by feeding the imagination.

out of love

If it all gets too weird, pick your moment to disengage. Leave him to his cravings in the hope that you will remain just good friends.

love lesson

Good sex is one thing, but good loving is everything.

activist

the archetype: The Hero, energizer, band leader, persuader and anarchist

the persona

how he appears to be

How to spot him – He'll be tied to a tree or asking you to sign a petition. He's the noisy one blaring at the party, going red in the face as he argues his point.

Dialogue / Verbal – Everything he says conveys his message as he hammers home his ideology or tries to win you round to his way of thinking.

Chat-line / Pick-up script – 'Are you free on Saturday? We need a big turnout.' 'Are you a spy?' 'Are you a rebel without a cause?'

Life course – To overrule opposition to what he believes in. To build his dream of the future. To gain support.

Accessories – Video footage, megaphone, paint, pager, disguises, lock pick, pocket binoculars, excellent memory, affiliated organizations, friends in high places, heroic stories for bedtime reading.

Day job – Political correspondent, photo journalist, politician, student, celebrity, union leader, legal-aid lawyer.

Babe history – No victims ... only volunteers. He takes no emotional hostages.

Theme song – 'Bring the Noise' by Public Enemy.

Fantasy – To return home to his second-in-command, his Cleopatra, bearing her off to his four-poster and there overwhelming her as the roar of victory still rings in his ears.

the shadow

who he really is

Bad habits – Aggressive behaviour, overbearing opinions, sexist attitudes, polarized thinking, obsessively loyal yet prone to character assassination. Avoids conflicting views, breaks rules and regulations, never forgets betrayal and wastes time on revenge.

What he doesn't say / Secrets and silences – 'Is the battle really worth the pain?'

Hidden agenda – To win in the face of adversity.

Philosophical mantra – The truth will be exposed.

Accessories – Safe places, code name, statistics, concealed camcorder, tape recorder, arrest sheet, slush fund, heavies, undercover agents, enemies, saboteurs.

Energy barometer – This guy has a fire in his belly. Lots of misdirected energy – it's what has sustained him for so long – and can be awesome at times. Sometimes he just cannot be quiet.

Relationship future – Get used to long goodbyes.

Theme song – 'All Along the Watchtower' by Jimi Hendrix.

Sex rating – He'll leave scorch marks on the sheets. If he thinks you share the same manifesto, his passion will rise to the fore. He's a Sherman tank in bed when he knows you're on the same side.

 6/10 5/10 6/10 8/10

aspects of the type

The Activist type has evolved from the fresh-faced, innocent idealist who wanted to change the world, right the wrongs, protect those in danger and save the environment. Life has been a tough task-mistress. He has not forgotten his lofty ideals or swapped them for political correctness. On the contrary, experience has given him an eagerness to perform in the political arena and he is now committed to campaign directly against those that oppose his ideals. He sees himself as the Motivator and his single-mindedness knows no boundaries. He is deeply committed to his chosen cause, whether it be political, religious, social or economic. His primary purpose is to challenge and eventually change decisions that impact upon our lives.

underhand methods. He'll try hard not to get mad, but to get even.

If he's a seasoned player, he handles difficulty with a cool head and diplomacy. He's learnt to be an ambassador for the cause he represents. Knowing that polemic will not always win people over, he has found other, lower-key ways to convince people from all walks of life. As someone who flies in the face of opposition he knows that sometimes he must schmooze, amuse and lose. He doesn't linger in self-pity for too long if he fails to take the cause a step further. His self-esteem must be strong to keep him motivated. It's this persistence that encourages those who join forces with him to be loyal, honest and bold.

His primary purpose is to challenge and eventually change decisions that impact upon our lives.

He is accustomed to dealing with arduous situations and he accepts that his actions must speak even louder than his words.

Confidence is not something this type lacks. He doesn't assume that everyone is going to agree with what he has to say and he is well practised at cutting through small talk. The man cannot tolerate insincerity and superficiality. He will always challenge propaganda. Never accepting what is presented to him at face value, he is quick witted, earnest and not so easy to fool. If he thinks that he's being taken for a ride, he may become ruthless, ushering in his own

If he comes across as a complex character, don't be put off. This may be an illusion. But his personality is riddled with contradiction: he claims to be fighting for the cause, to implement 'a better way'; it just so happens that it's also *his* way. Yes, there is a strain of the Activist in most men! He shields his personal life from the threat of intrusion by politics or power struggles. Alert to opportunities, he is always ready to interact with other Activist types, whose passion or protest he will either support or resist. Life is a fight. This guy sweetens his with plain old good intentions.

 7/10 . 4/10

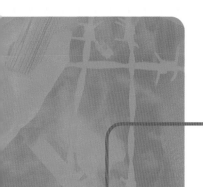

aspects of the soul

The twenty-first century Activist has to be creative to get his point across. And, in a world full of back stabbing, dishonesty and actual violence, the guy inevitably feels disillusioned and misrepresented at times. He must be a hopeful soul, or why would he continue the uphill struggle? That feisty spirit can tolerate a few knocks but he needs a constant buffer to stay buoyant. Whatever he needs, he finds it alone – energized by the quest to induce change. He is a believer in himself and in the cause he has chosen.

The Activist welcomes the diversity of his fellow agitators: activists span generations and cultures. What is common to them all is a desire for change and it's this characteristic that both frightens and informs others. Some see him as the Robin Hood of today's fast-moving world. He certainly gives everything to the cause: even his spirit has a campaign strategy. He is determined to get his message across, though this may call for radical action. And that is his dilemma: the price of justice may be peace.

Disruption for its own sake is not something that he necessarily enjoys. Not all Activists are extremists. Although he may take on the role of agitator and ringleader, he is better profiled as a reformer rather than a revolutionary. How far he will go to achieve reform depends entirely on the man. But whatever his choice, he will base his strategies and methods on heartfelt principles.

This is a man who has the ability to empathize, especially with the underdog, the unheard, the unseen, the unwanted. That yearning for justice lies deep down in the Activist's psyche, and it spurs him on to make a difference in the lives of others. He believes in people power as the proper instrument of direct action so he works hard to instill confidence, encouraging others to reject the unacceptable. As the voice of the people, he looks for concrete solutions to high-light the importance of civil liberty. He is anti-corporation, anti-multinational, sometimes anti-system. In his soul lies his mission: whatever it is, his commitment is profound.

He is a communicator in the heroic mould. The us-against-them mentality helps to forge strong bonds with like-minded individuals. His strength lies in the fact that he is not afraid of defeat. Any dilemmas that he might have will be overridden by a decisiveness based on integrity.

 5/10   7/10

in real life

the mindful citizen, whistle blower, religious fanatic, freedom fighter, environmentalist, feminist, volunteer worker for a non-profitmaking organization, spin doctor

the art of love

In love the Activist type is a restless spirit. You're looking at a guy that may be hard to pin down. He just loves to be on call, ready for action. He is a doer, capable of handling several projects at once. Prising him away from his beloved cause may be a thankless task. Forget a normal life: this guy is not a nine-to-fiver. His work life spills over into his private life. Time is not something he has a lot of and he certainly is not going to waste it. But so much of his life is unpredictable that he may be seeking a settled home life, where he can hide away from the pressure of protesting.

Love is his cause if he wants it to be. But this type only invites love if he is sure there'll be a spark. He is not prepared to indulge himself too often in pursuits of the trivial. He likes a woman of substance, and that raw masculinity cannot be resisted. He is good at what he does and being convincing is one of his talents. Most likely he will be able to charm you with his assertiveness and burning dedication to a cause. If he talks you into a date, be flattered – his time is precious.

Because the Activist is *au courant*, it's likely that he will be programmed to expect equality within a relationship. Debate is also something that he finds it easy to accommodate, and heated discussion between lovers can be great. But his investment in the right to think, choose and act independently may give him a sense of emotional superiority. This could make him mistrustful of a partner's intentions. If you don't agree with his ideals, beware of his disapproval. He will be resentful of those who dismiss the value of protest in an ever-changing world.

Used to being a part of a united force, he will want to enjoy the security of a tight partnership. Sharing the same vision of the future is therefore a must. He will need you to believe in him and what he stands for. Without mutual understanding and genuine agreement there will be no real respect.

His need to inform means that he will want any relationship to remain dynamic and frank. He is not the type to sweep problems under the carpet. He'll want them out into the open for discussion and resolution. In love the Activist will take promises seriously. He is a man of his word and dislikes having to change plans midstream. Most Activists will have radar tuned to pick up emotional manipulation. He has a low threshold when it comes to neediness, and he will automatically walk away from a demanding partner. Appreciating his ability to stay committed and empowered could lead to a solid foundation in love.

♥ 5/10   👁 4/10

into action / interaction

the hook

The Activist type will immediately be drawn to unabashed femininity. Be bold: show him what you're made of – it's not cotton wool. Draw him in by exercising your right to peaceful protest. He will respond to a woman who is not afraid to say what she feels. Base your argument in fact: he'll be impressed with your knowledge of civil liberties. Climb those barricades!

into love

Behind every great man there ought to be a great woman. Be ready to join the fun, holding his hand and marching in the front row with banners flying. Don't ignore how much he relies on your approval. This guy needs to feel supported, and the best way to do this is to value him. Above all, be unified.

out of love

If he's trying too hard to be Superman, he may leave you like Lois Lane – out of the frame. It's fine to have some unruly behaviour in your sex life but, if he proves an anarchist outside the bedroom, don't stand for it. He may just bore you to tears. Don't get in a lather – just leave him when he's not looking. He won't be able to resist the campaign to get you back!

love lesson

Getting through to this headstrong hero takes perseverance. He's accustomed to confrontation – why not speak softly to make yourself heard?

dr. feelgood

the archetype: The Altruist, new ager, mind-body-spirit man, attuned healer

the persona

how he appears to be

How to spot him – Find him at weekend warrior workshops, in a commune or on pilgrimage. He loves good energy so head for happy smiley parties, where throwbacks from the sixties still do their thing.

Dialogue / Verbal – Psycho-babble meets Woodstock. Softly spoken, he delivers his words as intensely as the day is long.

Chat-line / Pick-up script – 'This is Dr Feelgood. I am listening.'

Life course – To teach others how to be comfortable with themselves.

Accessories – Yoga mat, incense burner, shrine, sandals, guru, liquid echinacea, juicer and wheatgrass press, gravity boots, progress chart, combi van, dream catcher.

Day job – Naturopath, homeopath, herbalist, yoga or pilates teacher, therapist, meditation teacher, festival organizer, sweat-lodge chief, crystal healer.

Babe history – Previous life = commitment issues. This life = still looking for the perfect match. Next life = ready for the perfect match. Meanwhile enjoys long kisses.

Theme Song – 'Easy' by The Commodores.

Fantasy – He's a high priest on a lifelong magic-bus ride with a long-haired flexi soul-mate who's wearing nothing but a see-through caftan.

the shadow

who he really is

Bad habits – Morning ablutions, long nails, gets too blissed out and passes out, corrects your posture, fussy eater, becomes fanatical about detoxing and annoying encyclopedic knowledge of the mysteries of life.

What he doesn't say / Secrets and silences – 'I still don't get the meaning of life. God, I'd love a steak, medium-rare, with French fries.'

Hidden agenda – If I know me, then I will know you.

Philosophical mantra – This is my hobby, to make people happy.

Accessories – Nicotine patches, hangover cures, colonics, chillum and secret stash.

Energy barometer – This guy is a purist who wallows in how good it feels to be alive. He is touchy-feely. His balanced chakras (his energy centres) are his pride and joy.

Relationship future – He's choosy, and if in doubt he'll consult the Tarot.

Theme song – 'Satisfaction' by The Rolling Stones.

Sex Rating – He's hot in bed if he is able to re-centre himself after all that giving. Mr Emotional Fix-It needs time to explore your erogenous zones. Set the video.

 4/10   7/10   8/10   3/10

aspects of the type

Dr Feelgood is the consummate healer. His reality is founded on his skills of listening, interpreting and guiding. He calms the confusion of those that consult him. His confidence engenders hope. His intuitive observations inspire trust from others. His empathy softens the harshness of other people's reality. He knows how to make even the most afflicted person feel regarded. He casts light where there was darkness and love where there was pain. This type cares about those around him and promotes a positive outcome to life's events. His low tolerance of human suffering strikes a chord with his wish to make a difference.

anxieties when interacting in a group. He has let go of the basic need to be all things to all people, and his intentions are clear when allowing others to make their own decisions and come to their own conclusions. People are drawn to him and wonder why. He may have a beaming smile and he will certainly look you straight in the eyes when introduced. But key to his popularity are his good will and magnanimity. And that happiness springs from his philosophy of

He knows how to make even the most afflicted person feel regarded.

He is a true optimist who believes that positive thinking aids mental health and physical well-being. He sets goals to make life easier and more enjoyable. He strives to instill that awareness in others and attempts to practise what he preaches. Although he takes his responsibilities to other people seriously, he finds time for himself. He recognizes that his personal growth determines how well he is able to minister to others.

Dr Feelgood has unlimited energy. He is open and light-hearted, great fun to have around. He can handle other people's projections and

acceptance. He has decided to make the most of his life. In valuing what he has, he relaxes into himself and is content. Yet this guy doesn't have all the answers. Indeed, in encouraging people to challenge and change their own frailties, he must be reminded that he too is flesh and blood. Any guru can develop an inflated sense of ego – that pompous Dr Feelgood may have lost sight of his own teaching. A relationship is the best cure. Don't worry: a true Dr Feelgood is an altruist inspired by faith, hope and charity. Enjoy.

 6/10   8/10

aspects of the soul

This guy is an ancient soul in a modern world. He is a seeker, concerned with the journey of the soul. He sees life as miraculous and mysterious and his purpose is to help others answer life's biggest question, 'Who am I?' He may base his care and concern for others on psychological or spiritual beliefs, but he finds peace of mind within himself.

By acknowledging the fact that life is difficult, he frees himself from the escapist fantasy of a perfect world. He has learnt the power of action in his own life, as well as in the lives of those he counsels, by accepting the inevitable twists and turns of fate. As a free spirit, he jumps into the river of life and welcomes the challenges that await him. He sees life as perpetually changing, and transformation from lower to higher awareness is his goal. Never a navel gazer he does, however, relish odd moments of melancholy.

A Dr Feelgood type is very connected – he never loses sight of the correlation between mind, body and spirit. He sees his occupation as a vocation and wants to give back to the world in an holistic way. By removing negative self-talk and replacing fear with faith, he integrates logic and compassion in direct, effective communication. Expert in diplomacy and in caring for the human spirit, he strives to convince those that come to him for advice or teaching that there is always a choice and a way through difficulties. Much of his skill is intuition: he spends time tuning into other people and bringing out their strengths and resilience.

As a man who embodies humanity, he is able to govern and guide, helping others make the transition into a life that is more abundant. Being mindful and self-aware in his decision making, he finds an appropriate balance between personal ambition and generosity, and he looks for the same generosity to shine in others. This is a man who can teach us about the relationship between caring and prosperity.

 7/10   8/10

in real life
the man who loves to detox, self-help addict, amateur therapist, traveller turned shaman

the art of love

Dr Feelgood's emotional landscape is vast. He sees love in all its variety. He knows the difference between self-love and selfishness, and understands that self-love, founded on self-sufficiency, is necessary in any loving partnership. To quote Lord Goring in Oscar Wilde's *An Ideal Husband*: '... to love oneself is the beginning of a lifetime romance'. In love Dr Feelgood looks for inter-dependence rather than co-dependence. Inter-dependence promotes growth and flexibility in interaction. Co-dependents have unrealistic expectations of the emotional investment in any relationship. In this state both parties remain slaves to their emotions, imprisoned behind walls of fear, anger, shame and pain. Dr Feelgood looks for a mirror image of himself to supply his present needs, a balanced partner who can complement his character assets and defects. Because he has evolved to a state of independence and self-reliance, his most successful love match would be with a person of equal inner strength.

This is a man who is able to create and sustain meaningful partnerships, and to do so is very important to his long-term happiness. Because he places great significance on developing relationships of quality, this type may sometimes fall in love with the idea of the perfect relationship; he will want to be wrapped up in the radiance of a cosmic connection. He needs to allow a relationship time to develop and must be prepared to work at it. However, he understands the importance of honesty in love, and this is the key to sustaining intimacy. He recognizes the interplay of love and fear that underpins all human interaction, and he acknowledges that real love is not for the faint-hearted. He is not perfect by any means but his reference point is love, not fear. If there is disagreement, he will want to discuss it openly to resolve difficulty. When he is ready for love, he won't give up until he has found his soulmate.

 8/10  3/10

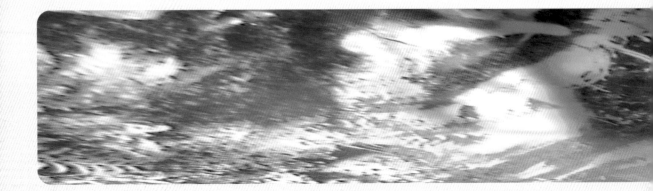

into action / interaction

the hook

He will be attracted by someone who is at ease with herself. Relax: leave your neurotic side at home. He is looking for a woman who takes care of herself in every respect. Keep yourself together; be communicative and expressive with your feelings. Invite him into the dance of mutual fascination.

into love

If this man makes your heart skip a beat, be sure to take the relationship seriously. This is a guy who will want to make the most of his time with you and will demand total commitment. He doesn't play games. Use your spiritual beliefs to strengthen your bond. Never forget that he is a special man: sensitive and insightful. Be true to him by always celebrating your love. Trust yourself and him equally.

out of love

Consider what you are giving up. Is it worth a second chance? Leaving him will be hard to do. Together you have experienced deep involvement. If your mind is made up, let him down gently. This type will take rejection personally. He is a sensitive and astute man who does not suffer fools gladly. Tell him how you feel immediately. Be as truthful as possible about your change of heart. He will need space and time to come to terms with it.

love lesson

We are all of us angels with only one wing. We can only fly by embracing each other.

media guy

the archetype: The Warrior, driven to win, creative absolutist, competitive sense of self

the persona

how he appears to be

How to spot him – He is at the epicentre of any social scene, his look-at-me stance shouts self-obsession. He is an air-kisser with high-octane, up-front energy and a babe-pulling smile; he's in control, on autopilot emotions, desperately seeking popularity. Performance is everything.

Dialogue / Verbal – Media speak, fluent in mid-Atlantic English, bilingual when pressed, nano-second networking, politically punchy, money talk: 'maxing the millions'.

Chat-line / Pick-up script – 'Do I know you, and if not why not?' 'Are you in the business?'

Life course – Born to win, again and again. Connections, connections, connections.

Accessories – Super-babe, sexy car, two mobiles, extra RAM in note-pad PC, show-reel and portfolio, latest club membership, travels business class whenever he can, the latest men's mags always at hand.

Day job – Film or music producer, radio DJ, award-winning advertising executive, A-List PR man, cutting-edge graphic designer.

Babe history – One in the background, one on the set, one he almost married and one he can never forget.

Theme song – 'Hanging On The Telephone' by Blondie.

Fantasy – The *Kama Sutra*, starring him with his favourite starlet massaging his world-weary soul.

the shadow

who he really is

Bad habits – Doesn't return your call fast enough, forgets to introduce you, calls you by another name and deserts you at parties.

What he doesn't say / Secrets and silences – 'I'm not free. I love my mother but I'm not the caring type. Will you look like this when you're fifty? One-to-one is not my forte.'

Hidden agenda – To find an independent, has-her-own-life woman. To continue subtle flirting even when in love.

Philosophical mantra – You get what you get.

Accessories – Martini meltdown, Bolivian oblivion, two kids from first marriage.

Energy barometer – Best guy to walk into a party with. Workaholic, perfectionist, stoic. His hyper-cycle often leads to end-of-deal meltdown.

Relationship future – She makes plans, he makes tracks. Time management needs work. Part-time sweetheart should be flexible with her diary. This is a guy disillusioned with superficial love. Catch him at the end of his career when he's ready to eject from the fast track and he'll be ready for forever after.

Theme song – 'Video Killed The Radio Star' by Buggles.

Sex rating – Too tired to shag. Weekends in the country needed for the real stuff.

 2/10   3/10   4/10   7/10

aspects of the type

This guy is brilliant, highly focused and creative. He is a natural competitor. His warrior persona protects him as he pursues fame and fortune. His desire for love and self-recognition drives him to work hard at success. Role models are fundamental to this type as they become *the* comparative, a benchmark of how he's doing. Status among his peers adds to the pressure that keeps him a lean, mean fighting machine. He knows all about the dangling carrot that holds him in the race. He probably put it there himself.

The need for his creative ideas and business proposals to be admired and applauded

The Media Guy has professional discipline. Up close and personal, however, it's not always the same story. By creating a busy lifestyle where the boundaries of work and play often overlap, he finds it hard to devote time to intimate relationships – which is exactly how he likes it. Much more fun to groove on down to the latest location and lose himself in the euphoria of the crowd. He is vivacious and flirtatious when he's up: the flip side to this is the perception that hits many media types who have been doing the scene for a while. Life literally becomes a sea of drowning faces at the ever-predictable première

> ## Status among his peers adds to the pressure that keeps him a lean, mean fighting machine.

is pivotal for the maintenance of his self-esteem. This sense of acceptance echoes a primal urge to honour his authentic self. His unconscious fear of not being good enough drives him into the realms of over-achievement. This guy will overcompensate and may exaggerate his past achievements and future potential. He has a perfectionist mind-set that reinforces his fear of inadequacy. He doesn't want to feel unworthy, and that is what he does feel when he is not able to do something he thinks he should be able to do. The idea of being a fake, of not being clever, unique or talented enough, can trigger disappointment. Unshakable confidence and self-doubt feed off each other in a cycle of highs and lows.

party or first-night gig. Unless he is careful to reserve time for himself and you, he will have little energy to put into the simple things in life.

A good way to harness his softer side, which could bring him the basic contentment he so yearns for, would be to encourage activities away from the madding crowd. His resistance to change will be daunting, but not insurmountable. He will rise to the challenge of intimacy as long as this does not conflict with prior engagements. The insecurities that are common in the Media Guy highlight his overweening pride so it may be a case of luring him into the subtler realities of love.

 6/10　　 8/10

aspects of the soul

The Media Guy drinks coffee in the morning. He's ready to go – out the door and heading for the car. He needs to get connected with the toys he has assembled. He wakes up feeling empty but by mid-morning he's speed dialling with a grin on his face. His book of days spills into nights. He is ambitious. His unrealistic goals raise his stress levels, resulting in controlled chaos. He juggles ten balls at once. He's in control and delivering. He meets his deadlines. Extreme conscientiousness is sourced from his hard-core perfectionist ideals.

Day-to-day business is an opportunity for dynamic self-expression: any situation can be worked to his advantage. His neediness centres around the desire for an eternal round of applause, of approval. Professional and artistic initiatives are set up as situations to win – opportunities for the lightning bolt of his competitive streak. Winning is everything: his motif, his *modus operandi*. All action is fuelled by an internal need for distraction. His spirit is veiled by the desire to achieve in the workplace. This is also true of the way he loves. High expectations put pressure on any partner and that is likely to drive her away.

Sadly, the anxiety created by his need to keep everything moving forward takes him away from the immediate situation. On many occasions he appears to be distracted. He is threatened when asked to give his total concentration to what might be happening in the here and now. He may be weakened by a fear of delving into his soul. He may even dismiss the concept of the search of the soul as sentimentality.

To effect change, the Media Guy will have to seek out some process by which he can contemplate the meaning of life. The first stage will be to build bridges between his interior and exterior worlds. This will require him to turn his thoughts inwards – something he consciously or unconsciously avoids in his working life. As a worker bee, his achievements always resonate immediately. More often than not his involvement in creative schemes will be as one of many contributors, and his comfort zone is made real by completing someone else's idea. He brings each project to fruition and then walks away. Upon completion responsibility ceases. The cycle of beginnings resumes and the opportunity for contemplation quietly escapes once more.

 3/10   5/10

in real life

the freelance hopeful, uncredited production crew, guest-list wannabe, film buff

the art of love

For the Media Guy the art of love is blocked by his fixation on perfection. It minimizes what he can contribute to any relationship. Self-conscious analysis plays such a central part in this guy's way of relating to other people that he becomes emotionally paralysed. He's so heady that he can't get hearty. He just doesn't know that it is OK to address imperfection.

It's by embracing the duality of who we are, our strengths and our weaknesses, that we become whole. When we are whole and at ease with ourselves, we discover a natural softness. This naturalness is the first requirement in loving and being loved, and its other name is attraction. It is this acceptance that the Media Guy needs to learn: he will eventually have to put down his sword and join the dance of life. This will mean being open to working with people for a communal outcome, working with a partner towards the same goal and being ready to let go and be taken into the complexities of what he has suppressed. He has a chance to see through his constant drive for attention as part of a like-minded set. He has the chance still to enjoy life in the fast lane, but with clarity.

By allowing himself to fall in love, he could experience integration of his outer self and his inner self. He is not a commitment phobic;

resistance to familiarity and routine have held him back. Emotional receptivity takes work – if it's too much like hard work he may lose the opportunity to articulate his own way of loving. This guy knows that life is not 'safe', yet he has made himself too safe by avoiding his own heart. In order to grow, the Media Guy has to rebuild trust in himself. Only then can he trust others and resolve the need to win, win, win. His aim in winning is to avoid defeat. It is arduous for this guy to accept that the spirit has no ulterior motive. Coming from a world of profile and ego, he finds it almost impossible to surrender to love. He has consciously to step out of the framework of his professional power base and into his other life: not quite as fast, not quite as guarded. Here there is scope for learning how to go with the flow.

This man has been raised to pursue ego goals, often without question. Such semi-predictable goals are cushioned by material security. True surrender with all its risks is experienced only on the path of love. The decision to remain on that safe level is always a possibility but the Media Guy will be a rewarding partner if he is willing to be led to a point of no return. That is, to move out of the limitations of 'I' into the expanded identity of 'we'.

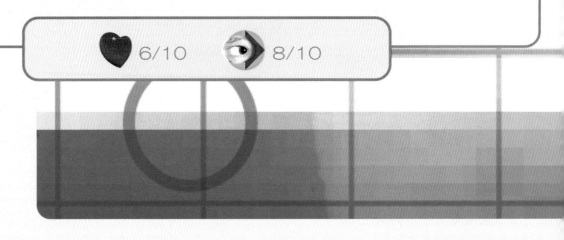

6/10   8/10

into action / interaction

the hook

His home-away-from-home is his favourite table at any of the must-be-seen restaurants opened this foodie fashion season. Follow the trends on after-dark hot-spots and you will find the Media Guy. Have a keen sense of who you are when you're around him. Appeal to his sense of style by being understatedly hip: 'current' stands for everything. Remember: making him look good counts. Kittenish behaviour should be put on hold for man-eating manoeuvres that will ensure attraction. This type has a short attention-span but his babe radar is never turned off.

into love

Be tough right from the start. There is potential for passion in the bedroom so have patience. All those late nights out may have depleted his stamina: be prepared to overwhelm him with a sensual touch. Your role may involve bringing a sense of balance into the relationship by harmonizing his work, social and personal commitments. Investing time in this strategy would be wise, as it will fire his sense of fun and playfulness.

out of love

Timing is everything. Pick your moment and be swift. Although he has failed to deliver the goods, this type has feelings, which he may turn on himself and descend into negativity. He may blame himself for not optimizing on love, a project he sees as problematic. Leave him with some hints on people skills, affirm his human potential and reassure him that defeatism is not the way. If he has let time slip through his fingers, let him see that commitment also has a place and a time, and in this case he missed the boat.

love lesson

Tell him honestly what you want, but be aware of the difference between aggression and assertiveness.

wanderer

the archetype: The Wanderer, free spirit, lone explorer, rolling stone, navigator

the persona

how he appears to be

How to spot him – Waiting for his flight to be called: his nonchalant attitude betrays the seasoned traveller. The wardrobe is an eclectic mix of garments from bazaars and bargain basements all over the planet. Style has become synonymous with individuality.

Dialogue / Verbal – Adopts the lingo of wherever he's passing through.

Chat-line / Pick-up script – 'Hey babe, swap seats with the bore so we can hang out for the long haul.'

Life course – To ride out into the unknown.

Accessories – Jesus sandals, beaten-up rucksack, one-man tent, billy can, hiking boots, e-mail address, needle and thread, camera, lucky charm, hand-made paper journal, Himalayan or Peruvian blanket, thermals, space food.

Day job – He's a counter-cultural dropout, which means that he works the season to save travel bucks.

Babe history – Occasional beauties add to the romance of the road.

Theme song – 'Black Magic Woman' by Santana.

Fantasy – To time-travel to Venus, where he is greeted by an all-female warrior clan who recognize him as the ancestor earth spirit returning home.

the shadow

who he really is

Bad habits – Disappears into thin air, calls collect, is always impoverished, leaves sand in the bed, empties the fridge and plans his next trip just as you're falling in love.

What he doesn't say / Secrets and silences – 'I only work for cash. I won't be around for long. I've got a girl in every port. Don't come with me.'

Hidden agenda – To escape the banal in everyday life. To avoid having to answer to anyone.

Philosophical mantra – In life we all walk alone.

Accessories – Rolling tobacco, sarong because he's a sexy dude, hand-picked T-shirt collection, iodine, dousing sticks, fake motorbike licence, false-bottom shoes, misled insurance broker.

Energy barometer – He's comatose, liming in the hammock, strung between two palm trees. When he needs to catch the plane, train or automobile, he's like lightning – usually running late.

Relationship future – Possible, but keep the gold band out of it.

Theme song – 'Nowhere To Run' by Martha Reeves and The Vandellas.

Sex rating – He's eager to prove his powers of sexual persuasion, which he does extremely well when there's a language barrier.

 2/10   1/10   7/10   3/10

aspects of the type

The Wanderer is the quintessential roving hero. In myth and legend he is the young knight who is driven out into the world by a tyrannical king or father and who finds a hidden treasure which he carries back to his homeland to lay triumphantly before the altar of the kingdom. In modern life it is authority that drives this type away. He is a non-conformist, acting out his distrust of whatever system, institution or person he feels undervalues his individuality.

young, because he has embraced his own life. He has attempted to free himself from the pressures of what other people think by making the decision to accept the lonely road. He's singular and he doesn't mind. He's finding out who he is by fleeing the nest and moving through the world. What he forgets is that you take yourself with you wherever you go.

Many people travel today but few make a life of it. The Wanderer will be more

The Wanderer will be more explorative in his travelling than others.

Often believing himself to be stereotyped and held captive in a rigid, false identity imposed by society's prevailing male role-models, he makes a crucial choice to experiment with other cultures in order to strengthen his sense of self.

This is a guy who does not place any faith in conventional solutions. But when he dismisses society's norms, he has to fill the space with some alternative way of living. Consequently he may live on the edge of society: not quite in the system, not quite outside it.

Dynamic and exciting to be around, he has made the assertion that life is not drudgery but a whopping, freewheeling, sexy adventure! This type will have a certain amount of maturity, even if he is

explorative in his travelling than others. For him it will be a quest. He will absorb the sights, sounds, smells and energies of the countries he visits and will feel comfortable in situations that others would find daunting. He will be ultra aware of what is going on around him and does not lose sight of what is important as he experiences the beauty and the ugliness of life. The wonderful thing about him is his ease with other people.

This type will learn to be self-sufficient and, although he chooses freedom, in time he often returns to play an active role in society. He will remain spontaneous and quick thinking, with a strong sense of identity, purely because he made a commitment to do what he wanted.

 5/10   8/10

aspects of the soul

The Wanderer loves solitude. The guy creates extreme 'aloneness' in order to grow. Paradoxically, as a Wanderer, going wherever his feet take him, his survival depends upon his flexibility. He must master the arts of adaptation, finding his place in all kinds of unfamiliar and strange surroundings.

This type may appear selfish: he certainly does not always take other people's feelings into consideration. But it is more accurate to say that he is a man who will not accept traditional morality simply for the sake of it. Instead of bending to the pressure to conform and mimic society's standards of living and loving, he prefers to create his own morality. The quest for self-definition is what drives him on. This man is daring – both in his exploration of the external world and in his own internal world. He turns away from those he is close to in pursuit of self-realization, drawing conclusions directly from his own experience and finding true vision through the dark night of the soul.

To follow his longing to travel, he relinquishes the role of provider, temporarily or permanently, and he jeopardizes his economic status and his friendships. The desire for material success is replaced by a thirst for the variety and richness that is OUT THERE! But society often sees the way in which he seeks to answer his questions about life as a cop-out. He is told that he is no use to anyone, that he is a dreamer. And such criticisms may be keenly felt. In particular, the sense of shame attached to non-achievement in the western world can undermine him.

In truth the Wanderer falls short only when he sacrifices intimacy for self-reliance. This type may have repressed his need for love and commitment because he thinks it will infringe his independence. Not true. He can have both. No man is an island, as the poet John Donne said, and the Wanderer's illusion that he can structure a life around the belief that he is reliant only on himself is slowly shattered when he realizes how scared he is of being abandoned by someone he loves. If he loves, that is. He may also believe that independence is a romantic asset, the ultimate symbol of masculinity. Only when he feels the sadness and alienation that this brings to his life will he be ready to change.

 6/10   7/10

in real life
the fruit picker, jewellery maker, seasonal sports coach, tree planter, festival fly pitcher

the art of love

To say this type is searching for himself wherever he journeys may be only half the story. He is also travelling in search of true love. Deep down, he has set a candle burning with the question, 'Where are you?' His dream is that she too is travelling the planet, and that some unknown force will eventually unite them.

When he is alone, he can feel – if he allows himself – the despair of loneliness. This is the moment when everything slips away. The security net is not in place and he comes face to face with the primal urge to fall in love and to experience what love brings to life. He has two choices. The first is to make himself available for love so that when he meets the right woman he will recognize her. The second is to let the moment pass and go grab a cup of *chai* from the teahouse down the street. If the Wanderer learns this lesson, he can be an incredible partner. When the time is right, he will follow his heart with the same conviction that he gave to his travelling. And he will see partnership as a lifelong journey on which both can experience what being together is all about.

When he has resolved the conflict between love and the need to be independent, this type will no longer feel separation. And his self-imposed isolation will no longer serve a purpose. He has put himself first and realized his dreams so he is free to allocate a place for loving in his life. But the impulse to remain as unencumbered as possible is very strong in him. He can be an unconventional romantic, contradicting any of the established acts of romantic love, but try to undermine his uniqueness and he will sting you like a scorpion. He has to feel that his place in the community is as a true individual. Once he asserts himself in a relationship, he will not feel threatened by it.

The Wanderer will always be a guy with a taste for the unknown. He will need you to share his delight in foreign cultures and his understanding of different ways of living. Give up any hope of a completely normal lifestyle and join him on the road, never knowing where the next bend will take you.

♥ 5/10   👁 6/10

into action / interaction

the hook

Book yourself into the same compartment on the sleeper bound for Shangri-la. The best way in is to tempt him with your supply of yum yums. Make him a food parcel and he will be grateful. Look cool and completely self-assured. Make out you are a hardened traveller and use all your Girl Guide skills to impress him. Next day set off together. Collect wood, make a fire, cook a three-course dinner in one pot, offer to row the boat ... Failure just won't come into it!

into love

If all is going well, keep in the moment. Relish the present and don't scare him off by making plans. Encourage him to enjoy being settled. Home is a state of mind more than anything else. If he's a roamer, travel together. Above all, allow him to make decisions about how he wants his life to be. Don't try to impose your own dreams. If it's meant to be, your dreams will be the same.

out of love

If you tire of having to bring him down to earth and being the stabilizer in the relationship, let him know. If together you can't strike a balance, let go of trying. Perhaps in your case he prefers to be solo. Don't book an outbound ticket. Sit out the pain at home. It will pass.

love lesson

Vibe him out before you vamp him. And don't let him seduce you if he's not hanging around for the full enchilada.

lad

the archetype: The Innocent, king kid, creature of habit, reliant on peer approval

the persona

how he appears to be

How to spot him – Follow the wolf whistle, check the scaffolding, peer down the manhole, honk in reply to the petrol-heads in the lane beside you.

Dialogue / Verbal – Chauvinist mumble, oy oy aye aye, wink wink nudge nudge, rhyming slang, loud and proud when lager fuelled. And he spins yarns.

Chat-line / Pick-up script – 'I'm organizing a wet T-shirt competition – you look like you could win.' 'Why don't you swap your bicycle saddle for me!' 'Can't you take a joke?'

Life course – Doesn't give a XXXX.

Accessories – Football kit, singlet, designer jeans, remote control, pool table, dart board, forgiving parents, autographed rugby ball, souped-up car, barbecue, play station, local pub, weekend wad, childhood sweetheart.

Day job – Unskilled to skilled: from banker to construction worker.

Babe history – Georgie Porgie, pudding and pie, kissed the girls and made them cry.

Theme song – 'My Way' by Sid Vicious.

Fantasy – Simultaneous viewing in a Vegas hotel: on the 3m flat-screen TV – the World Cup; in the mirrored ceiling – sexual antics performed on him by a blonde babe scoring 10 out of 10. Open packet of crisps for afterwards, washed down with a half of brew.

the shadow

who he really is

Bad habits – Flashes his arse, burps and breaks wind loudly and frequently, shovels food, never puts the loo seat down, adds tomato ketchup to everything, thinks staring is flirting, is fanatical about sports and has wandering hands after a few beers.

What he doesn't say / Secrets and silences – 'Can my mates come on the honeymoon? I miss my mum – she's the best cook.'

Hidden agenda – To keep his roving eye busy and pass loud comment on passing women.

Philosophical mantra – If it ain't broke, don't fix it.

Accessories – Big bar bill, big belly if big telly, can coolers, burnt frying pan, late-night curries (hotter the better), hangover cures, soft-porn videos, pin-ups, souvenir ashtrays, disposable razor, soap on a rope.

Energy barometer – Roaring at the game, peaking at the pub and out for the count when horizontal. Non-existent when he's over-dosed on nights in with a take-away. Can become sloth-like and lazy.

Relationship future – He will have one night a week free for you. Be warned: he is economical emotionally.

Theme song – 'Wonderwall' by Oasis.

Sex rating – He humps at night. Don't look for love in the afternoons.

 9/10   5/10   5/10   8/10

aspects of the type

His spark of adolescent male bravado remains throughout his life. This type is happiest when he is with his buddies. For him, the pressure to create a façade or project an image is irrelevant. He doesn't give a toss about what others think of him – 'others' meaning anyone outside his pack.

interest. He loves to veg out on the couch at home, with a few mates, a lot of beer and his trusty remote control. Life is sweet. He is unfazed by opportunity. He'll take career moves that match his down-to-earth lifestyle: deviating from his routine is not something that appeals.

He is loyal to those he loves and this extends to his mates.

He gravitates towards a group in which he can be himself. He's a big kid, and he wants an easy life. He knows his place in society and accepts where he's at with ease. He can be found in every social strata: what sets him apart is his willingness to tow the line. He is not the type of guy that wants to make waves. There is a certain comfort in knowing where he has come from and there is reassurance in the fact that his parents have not pressured him to outclass or outsmart them. But if he were to want to better himself, he would be supported, 100 per cent. He is loyal to those he loves and this extends to his mates. He forms life-long friendships. His easy-going temperament is a simple case of what-you-see-is-what-you-get.

The sports calendar provides the highlights of his life and going to the game is his seasonal routine. He'll support the team: be it cricket, rugby, football or whatever grabs his

He is territorial and macho. He may be highly opinionated and that can turn negative when life or traffic doesn't move as it should. He is easily angered by insults, real or imagined, and then his passivity flips into aggression. Self-righteousness may also provoke misdirected

outbursts when he does not get his way and this will attract antagonism. But just as quickly as his temper flares, he gets over it. There is a little of the Lad in almost all men. Boys will be boys.

 4/10   3/10

aspects of the soul

He may once have been a choir boy, but you won't find the Lad in the lotus position, searching for the key to enlightenment. This may be to his benefit in a spiritual sense. Because he does not complicate his life with existential questions about the whereabouts of a higher power, he sees life objectively and practically. And, in consequence, he turns to himself for a sense of meaning and value.

It does not take much to awaken his spirit. He may be crude and brash, unthinking and tactless, but his heart is very genuine and he can be motivated by kindness. There's nothing he wouldn't do for someone he cares about – be it his granny or his next-door neighbour. This is a good bloke, the type you'd call on when you'd locked yourself out. It is just the initial getting to know him that is daunting.

His mates are of profound importance to him. Together they form a mutual admiration association. And for the Lad, the group acts as a safety net. Camaraderie, humour and cheekiness are the coping skills he falls back on time and time again. He takes the rough with the smooth but he tends to bottle up his feelings. He would hate to be seen as a sensitive type, and so he may be homophobic. Ironically, his strong male bonding directly parallels aspects of the homosexual world. Equally, with the advent of women's economic independence and the crisis in male identity, many heterosexual men have been impelled to seek ways of returning to their masculinity in the kind of affinity groups traditionally associated with the Lad type.

This guy does not look into himself with ease. His friends do not ask it of him and nor does he ask it of himself. That would be a big step for this almost innocent man. His is the k.i.s.s. philosophy – 'Keep it simple, sweetie'. For him prayer is a pint and meditation is deep sleep. Satisfaction for the Lad comes from stability. He is caring and encouraging, often homebound, and definitely a creature of habit.

 4/10 5/10

in real life

the cheeky window cleaner, regular at the social club, joker, refuse collector, car salesman, Friday and Saturday night clubber, milkman

the art of love

When the Lad wants to shoot the breeze, he will opt for his mates. The average woman uses considerably more words than the average man per day; the Lad uses considerably less than either and, if by the end of the day he has run out of words, he won't want to exert himself. Male time is a safe option for a guy who is in no hurry to exercise his feminine side. His mates won't confront him, harass him into disclosure or jostle him into performing.

This type is hard work on the love front. He is the fly-by-night type, more or less happy with casual relationships until his friends start settling down. He finds it hard to interpret and satisfy the emotional needs and desires of women. He does not want to deal with the resentment he stirs up because of his emotional inadequacy so he puts space between himself and any partner, becoming distant and unresponsive.

Withdrawing and withholding are also sure signs that he is mulling things over. He does not find relief in talking through his own problems, which will always be mundane, day-to-day matters, and he feels threatened and concerned if he is unable to handle another person's problems. At base, he is scared of disappointing others. To unwind, he reads the sports pages or watches TV. He can feel his anxieties dissipate as the game unfolds, and this is why sport is so important to him.

 4/10   8/10

into action / interaction

the hook

Be a ladette. Be the cheerleader to his team. Be tough. Break the ice by buying him a beer. If you want sex that night, buy him a bag of pork scratchings. Show him legs and cleavage; he's a tits-and-bum man. Look like you can hold your drink. Never embarrass him in front of his friends. Ask him out, but to get the best response do it in private. Tell him you love him just the way he is.

into love

Put the kitten mules aside and be ready to fetch and carry. Don't ask questions, don't make demands, don't criticize and don't have expectations. Cook meat and two veg. on a Sunday. Offer to organize a girls' night out when his mates come round. Show him the multiplicity of love: be a chef in the kitchen, a lady in the living room and a whore in the bedroom. His curiosity will be aroused. Never ask him to go shopping with you.

out of love

Had enough of cooking, cleaning, fetching and carrying? Pack up your pots and pans and leave. He is used to relationships that end so there is little chance of him coming after you. Be brave. Change drinking holes.

love lesson

Enjoy being young, but don't expect anything to change.

philosopher

the archetype: The Lover, meaning seeker, life examiner, trapped in a thought

the persona

how he appears to be

How to spot him – You will hear him before you see him. He is not a careful dresser and comes across as animated and intense with an array of gestures to reinforce his old-style debating technique. He will take you hostage if you play mind games with him.

Dialogue / Verbal – Excitable when trying to prove his point, clever and witty, light-hearted, cynical if he's in one of his black moods.

Chat-line / Pick-up script – 'Who are you? I'd like to know what makes you tick.' 'How do you define love?' 'Would you like to know the meaning of Life?'

Life course – To question existence again and again and again.

Accessories – Smoking jacket for periods of deep rumination, pipe, spectacles, dog-eared books, teach yourself Ancient Greek cassettes, fountain pen, satchel, well-worn best leather shoes, very comfortable armchair, chess set.

Day job – Writer, researcher, lecturer, crusading journalist, social commentator.

Babe history – Only students of his school of thought get a look-in.

Theme song – 'Imagine' by John Lennon.

Fantasy – To seduce all female philistines, time travelling back and forth through the centuries with Aphrodite, goddess of Desire, at the helm of the *Cult of Logic*.

the shadow

who he really is

Bad habits – Doesn't look at you when he speaks, picks his nose and mutters.

What he doesn't say / Secrets and silences – 'I'm terrifically boring. I'm trying to make sense of it all. My best thinking time is loo time. My head-space is sacred. I never dust.'

Hidden agenda – To be taken seriously.

Philosophical mantra – An unexamined life is not worth living.

Accessories – Biscuit tin and teapot, garden shed, video games for when he gets brain overload, the complete works of Plato.

Energy barometer – This guy is so used to contemplating the meaning of existence that he really can't be bothered to do much else. But he compensates for the lack of physical presence by reading you poetry and interesting newspaper cuttings.

Relationship future – Desperate. This chap is forever analysing the chemistry of romance in hope of a piece of the action.

Theme song – 'The Dark Side Of The Moon' by Pink Floyd.

Sex rating – It's a mental orgasm he's burning for – not a genital one! Put your toga on and combine the two.

 6/10   7/10   5/10   3/10

aspects of the type

The Philosopher is an introvert with little need for external stimulation. His framework of beliefs and expectations leads him to study the processes of thought and the meaning of life. He is inspired by the arts, psychology, literature and the classics: you might see him at the museum, checking out the ancient manuscripts, or in the library, reading philosophers like Aristotle or Jean-Paul Sartre.

He experiences himself as different from other people, and he's right. There aren't so many of them about. He lives in a world of concepts. Information is acquired to defend his inner world. Arguments are mapped out and articulated to bring the outside world under control. He is a talented speaker: insistent and flexible in his approach, good at bringing an audience round to his way of thinking. You'll hear the cogs of his brain spin and whirr while you chat to him. He's got superb critical powers. It's only unfortunate that he doesn't always translate them into action. He prefers ideas and theory to implementation. In many ways he is very much a dreamer. Happy to live in his dreams because they all make perfect sense.

The Philosopher type is fun to have around if he doesn't become too melancholic. This is a man full of suggestions about how to live life. They literally trip off his tongue. Find him in the coffee houses by day and at the local by night; look again at that solitary man feeding the ducks in the park. He might be alone but he is never afraid to strike up a conversation with almost anyone who's willing. He's not picky. He doesn't believe he is superior, though he may want you to come round to his way of thinking. He's looking for an admirable character like himself to team up with. He is not greedy and doesn't find material acquisition that stimulating. He is thoughtful and caring. Whatever he has, he will share with you.

> ## He experiences himself as different from other people, and he's right.

 7/10 5/10

aspects of the soul

He is a believer. Truth is his absolute, rather than any god or higher power. His search for the meaning of life is constantly measured against that absolute. He loves to be rational and analytical. This guy lives in a self-created world. Understanding the very roots of religion, society, culture and love is fundamental to him. He is full of ideas, theories and, in some cases, adventure. He loves to make plans and envisages a bright future ahead of him in his hungry pursuit of truth. Anticipation leaves him keenly disappointed when things fall through, but his capacity to recuperate emotionally is self-sustaining, and his passions are conceptual rather than felt. Living in his mind produces the illusion of non-attachment.

This man has few emotional needs or possessions. Material wealth is not prized as highly as philosophical understanding. This really turns him on. It is his singular goal.

He enjoys making and breaking his own belief system. He justifies his constant changes or adaptations of outlook as the inevitable response to new or revised information. His pursuit of truth is contained within strong moral and ethical values but he plays devil's advocate when considering the rationality of good and evil. He sees the narrow space separating the two as the springboard for all human potential. Social philosophers are charitable, politically driven and love to teach or be in the limelight. Idealistic philosophers perceive life in a more intuitive and profound way, being more passionate and more concerned with the spiritual aspect of life. Both strive to live in an idealized world and are fascinated by the notion of cosmic order and the origins of the universe.

The Philosopher recognizes that there are timeless principles which guide the passing show we call life. The irony is that this guy needs a signpost to find his spirit. And he will see that only when he frees himself from constant mental activity by renouncing his investment in analysing all that is around him.

 6/10   8/10

in real life
the cosmologist, social anthropologist, pontificator, agnostic, drunk at the bar

the art of love

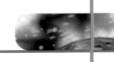

The Philosopher longs to be touched by others. He wants to live out what he feels within his interior world of questions and concepts. Attracted to people that are interested and interesting, he seeks to gather all the strands of his fragmented self, binding them together in the understanding of true love. He dreams of living a life connected to his inner world, through feelings, and to his outer world, through his relationships with people. He is stimulated by the ancient classical myths of creation, by Eros, for example, who is seen as a personification of the drive to unite passionate and romantic love, that universal, unconscious need for fusion, completeness, wholeness.

The Philosopher type seeks always to be charming. He is often romantic, though there are sceptics in the ranks. In love he looks for the bolt of lightning. He awaits a woman who will dazzle him with her integrity and flexibility of thought. He wants a refined mind that he can tinker with. Being in a relationship will lighten him up and give him a reason to live in his feelings rather than his head. But the thinking type can be troubled by what he doesn't understand. Never at peace with what he knows, he seeks to know more. This makes him inquisitive in love.

If he becomes truly enamoured, intellect is bypassed for this new lust and devotion. Wonderment shifts from facts to feelings. Ignorance is seen as the only evil so watch out for his possessiveness. He will want to know everything about you and may find it hard to accept that things are simple and straight-forward, even when they are. Idealism seeps away as he slips into the lower plain of consciousness and becomes human and just like everyone else. For the Philosopher to access love on the higher plain, he must feel the joy of love as well as its pain and poignancy. When he does, this guy can take you to the fourth dimension, the dimension of time. His state of bliss will be fired by a partner who can accept and share his abstractions.

♥ 7/10   5/10

into action / interaction

the hook

The guy likes to be listened to. He has a caustic humour. Challenge him with your wit. This lonesome dove will be so subtle in love you'll need to be a detective to read his clues. Be gentle. He may be opinionated but you can bet your bottom dollar he suffers from shyness. He will be more enthralled by a woman with a curiosity for life than a glamour puss.

into love

The Philosopher is an interesting companion rather than a passionate lover. He'll make a fantastic friend and this is a good basis for a loving relationship. Be careful not to violate his values. If you are more of an extrovert than him, be aware of his introversion. Consider the difference in energy levels, especially in a social setting. Above all, establish a strong rapport with your man before you debate controversial topics. This type hates to be disagreed with; harmony is the way forward.

out of love

If he won't let you go, annoy him by talking too much, dumbing down your theories on life and invading his quiet time and privacy. You will drive him mad. It's easy to remain friends with a Philosopher type – there'll be a history of shared, meaningful ideas. But head for the door if his scepticism casts gloom on the future.

love lesson

The longest journey is from the head to the heart.

uniform man

the archetype: The Hero, confronts danger, respects hierarchy, carries responsibility

the persona

how he appears to be

How to spot him – He's a give-away unless he's undercover. Find him behind enemy lines, in a war zone, at the crime scene, saving lives or rescuing cats from trees.

Dialogue / Verbal – A man of fewer words than most, his megaphone tones and clear articulation instill order and discipline. His bark is worse than his bite.

Chat-line / Pick-up script – 'I'll let you off with a warning this once. Now, how about dinner?'

Life course – To feel he is of use. To maintain the status quo.

Accessories – Shiny boots, stripes, bullet-proof vest, regulation leather trousers, camouflage, reflective clothing, helmet or hat, hair clippers for no.1 haircut, hose, truncheon, ammunition, Swiss Army knife, the kiss of life.

Day job – Fireman, policeman, military man serving in the armed forces, paramedic, air and sea rescue, security guard.

Babe history – In the past he has had to fight them off with a stick – he moves quickly when alarm bells sound.

Theme song – 'Heroes' by David Bowie.

Fantasy – To respond to the call of duty, save the world and come home to his choice page 3 pin-up in uniform and suspenders, ready for the striptease.

the shadow

who he really is

Bad habits – Swears big time, over-disciplines the puppy, mistakes dancing for marching, forgets to take his uniform off after work and gets grumpy when he's working nights.

What he doesn't say / Secrets and silences – 'No, I'm busy' to a damsel in distress.

Hidden agenda – To have his authority respected. To be a force to be reckoned with. To be highly regarded within the community.

Philosophical mantra – Honour is the first and last calling.

Accessories – Crisis counsellor, hip flask, suppositories, knuckle duster, action-hero videos, nudes on locker door, training schedule, iron, starch, battle souvenirs, letters from the home-front.

Energy barometer – He's hard to handle when the adrenaline has been pumping. Cool-headed in a crisis, he shifts gear to raise temperatures between the sheets.

Relationship future – If you can't take the heat, then get out of the kitchen. Shift work and time away from home put pressure on relationships.

Theme song – 'If Everybody Looked The Same' by Groove Armada.

Sex rating – Be realistic but hopeful. Maximum energy + minimum anxiety = the Big Bang. Hand-picked, he's an officer and a gentleman.

 6/10   6/10   7/10   9/10

aspects of the type

The Uniform Man lives his life by the rules. They ensure his place in society. He is expert at the restoration of law and order and derives enormous satisfaction from a job well done. His extraordinary ability to act now and ask questions later is absolute.

He places a high value on discipline and has had to challenge his basic instincts to survive the rigours of training: breaking down his weaknesses and building up his strengths has paid off in situations where the odds are against him. He is a fierce opponent in a constant state of alertness with a highly developed sense of survival, and his exceptional courage allows him to act effectively in the face of adversity. When a threatening situation arises, he automatically puts the safety of others before his own.

expectations. He may try to view life as a struggle in which the victims emerge safe and he is the victorious protector. But who is minding the minder? This type's integrity is constantly being challenged or violated by circumstance. How well he balances his experience and remains compassionate and non-judgmental will depend upon his emotional strength.

To some this dilemma becomes a constant preoccupation. If he is inclined to feelings of guilt, he will brood on how he could have acted more effectively, and this internalization will be self-defeating. The guy needs to see the benefits of getting to know himself at a deeper level. Probing his reactions with the same intensity he gives to his work will serve him better than an

His extraordinary ability to act now and ask questions later is absolute.

He has shed any illusions about his chosen profession being 'just a job'. Instead, he is realistic about the dark side of human nature and the violent manifestations of man's inhumanity to man. The inner conflict between right and wrong does exist for the Uniform Man. He values a moral and honest approach to life. He strives to remain uncorrupted by keeping his own counsel.

How he makes sense of the chaos and carnage will alter his perceptions and his

unrealistic self-image in the long run. Although he takes life soberly when he needs to, his sense of humour is primed to reduce the tension in his moments of crisis.

He is trained to work within a unit, and it is there to support him. Being a competent team member is also important if he wants to climb the career ladder. But self-motivation is an inherent part of keeping morale high and team spirit alive.

 5/10 5/10

aspects of the soul

The Uniform Man attempts to make sense of the love and hate he witnesses day by day. His experience has repeatedly shown him that there is need for kindness, that death and destruction must be succeeded by restoration and renewal. This is key to his existence: he could not function without the belief that life can be improved upon. It is this that pushes him into battle.

Watching him from a distance in the hardest of times illustrates how he self-protects in a tricky predicament: he can separate mental threat from physical danger in a violent world. But don't be taken in. He carts the emotional aftermath home in the recesses of his mind. He has more experience of the fragility of the human condition than most: more knowledge of the desperation, the shock, of lives turned inside out. He acknowledges that pain and suffering are inevitable, and the cost is a loss of innocence. If he were to deny it, he would have to become cynical to cope.

The Uniform Man may struggle with other people's perception of him. He knows that he must change his style and language to suit each individual. The democratic notion that interacting with everybody in the same way, regardless of rank or status, makes him a model citizen is dismissed.

This is a man who has to deal with overt power plays from those he contacts. Many feel alienated, anxious and suspicious of authority. As a keeper of order, he has to reassure people by demonstrating how action will benefit them. Sometimes he uses tact and persuasion to get what he wants. But his training has also taught him the value of boldness. Boldness disguises timidity and sustains the illusion of power. This apparent self-confidence both attracts and repels other people. Yet the psyche of this type runs on approval and acknowledgment; behind the badge there lies a hungry ego which has to be fed. He needs to be respected and to respect his peers and seniors. Implicit in any perception of hierarchy are subordination, responsibility and some degree of conformity.

3/10   6/10

in real life

the member of the TA or British Legion, bouncer, traffic warden, male nurse

the art of love

He is a defender of the faith. Full of intentions to do good and preserve the fabric of society, he is blind to the politics of control and domination. The widely held view that very few individuals can use power peacefully is effectively blocked because Uniform Man types recognize the need for a belief system that justifies the cause. To fight the enemy you must believe that you are defending what is right: the end can then justify the means. But not everyone shares this opinion so he finds himself applauded by most sections of the community, ostracized by a few. If he has felt society's rejection, his heart may be hardened.

This guy is tough on the outside, soft and vulnerable within. He may deflect love, struggling to keep people who care at a safe emotional distance. Trained to negate the emotional reactions that can obstruct the task at hand, he is hard to reach. He feels the need to control his surroundings, to take time to readjust after the drama of his day, and yet this expert at restoring control may have a secret wish to break free from all restraints. At a more basic level security in a relationship is a must for him. He is a man that requires structure in every aspect of his life: outside some framework he feels threatened.

He is aware of the effect he has on women. By some he is regarded as a powerful protector. They have a field day with the fantasy of a man in uniform: he can be sexually objectified or idealized as a homage to masculinity. Either will spark his heroic fantasy of himself: a stud, invincible, totally irresistible and underneath this male machismo – a heart. In reality, he is not good at being emotionally present. He tends to switch off when asked to contribute his inner feelings. Criticism is also hard to take, and he may play the tough guy to prevent you getting through the chinks in his armour. He has to readjust to allow space for intimacy in a relationship. But, despite his fight-or-flight response to love, he can benefit from true companionship.

 6/10   9/10

into action / interaction

the hook

Show your legs, even if it's winter! Cry for help and look desperate. He loves to feel needed and that he's running the show. Let him believe it. Nod and smile. He'll be on the lookout for a woman with a twinkle in her eye, someone who brings out the rebellious side of him. Light his fire with flames of sweetness. He needs a lot of reassurance: behind the gallant façade is a man keen to do his best.

into love

Make home a wonderful place to return to. Don't be worried if his need to control is overwhelming: you can teach him new tricks. You will need to comfort him if he is despondent. His commitment to his work can be excessive at times. Make sure your two worlds don't collide – his is virtually immoveable. Be his rock of support. He'll respond with gratitude.

out of love

Don't leave a forwarding address!

love lesson

Throw out his rule book. Design your own code of conduct, making love not war.

recovering addict

the archetype: The Hero, wounded orphan, survivor, Icarus on his flight to the sun

the persona

how he appears to be

How to spot him – You never can tell.

Dialogue / Verbal – He's hard to decipher for those not initiated into the format of recovery speak. He loves to sound deeply psychological, which may leave you deeply confused.

Chat-line / Pick-up script – Alcoholic = 'Want to go for a drink?' Not! Sex addict = 'I hope you don't mind me mentioning it, but your panty line is showing.' Drug addict = 'Did you say you were fine or would I like a line?' Co-dependent = 'Coffee, tea or me?' (Pick me, pick me!)

Life course – To set up home on the edge of the cliff.

Accessories – 12-Step Meeting List, sponsor, psychoanalyst, AA buddies, mirror, vitamins, water bottle, new-lease-of-life smile, inspiration cards, punch bag.

Day job – The show must go on and, given the chance, he'll shine again.

Babe history – An ex-wife who never knew him and a new companion who is trying to.

Theme song – 'Golden Brown' by The Stranglers.

Fantasy – Alcoholic = to be a social drinker. Sex addict = to be reincarnated as a rabbit. Drug addict = to grow a mainline orifice. Co-dependent = to be reincarnated as a Siamese twin.

the shadow

who he really is

Bad habits – Pours his heart out over dinner and takes ages to lighten up. Dumps you for a newcomer to the group.

What he doesn't say / Secrets and silences – 'Rescue me. Don't ever leave me. If I fool you, you'll do.'

Hidden agenda – To justify being a control freak. To manipulate misunderstandings with newly discovered insights. To have his feelings take priority over yours.

Philosophical mantra – Live life on life's terms.

Accessories – Sunglasses, mints, crisis-line number, chocolate bars, unopened recovery books, heal-your-inner-child tapes, unloved teddy bear, dysfunctional family, criminal record.

Energy barometer – Verbally, he could go for 24 hours. Physically, life knocks him out by 10 pm. Emotionally, it's better when he's been to a meeting.

Relationship future – Not in the first year, darling.

Theme song – 'Walk On The Wild Side' by Lou Reed.

Sex rating – Re-awakened lust makes for a safe bet between the sheets. He's aware of his feelings and yours.

 5/10  2/10   6/10   6/10

aspects of the type

It's a long road home for the walking wounded. This is a rare species who gets to have two lives: one he wished he never had and one he has yet to live. He escaped from the shallow end of the gene pool, vowing never to be like his addictive parent, but history has a peculiar way of repeating itself. For years he believed he was unique and special. Ordinary life was eschewed: people were there as enablers, to be used for his addiction. Now his dream is to rewind life's tapes and do it differently. But he must carry his lost years in his inside jacket pocket: they never leave him. Haunted by the past, loaded with complicated sentiment, his mind is in constant

lover, cancelling the void of feeling. Why? Because life was so damn hard. The only escape was death, and this was far too frightening. So he tried another way, failing to see that spiritually it results in the same thing. Addiction made him numb. It allowed him to run from every genuine feeling he ever had and halted his emotional growth. Addiction: the slow route to death.

He has chosen to stop feeding his addiction. And then to stay stopped.

turmoil. Addiction is a mental obsession as well as a physical compulsion. It would be so easy to slip into old patterns and relapse.

    What makes this type so significant is his decision to save his own life. He has chosen to stop feeding his addiction. And then to stay stopped. Having made the choice, he has to fight temptation for ever, one day at a time. This guy comes into recovery with little self-worth and, by altering his attitudes, discovers a new confidence. Addiction had played the role of

    The Recovering Addict is a man in transition. His saving grace is that at some point he recognized the void of his own life. He understood that there were no answers, never had been, and that everyone's in the same boat. So he swallowed his pride and came face to face with the demons that he had created. He surrendered to start winning.

 6/10   3/10

aspects of the soul

This man has fallen, and in space no one hears you scream. His fall began in disillusion and ended in desperation. Excess had a part to play in his past. Self-indulgent and naïve, he fed too long on the temptations of the world, not recognizing the consequences of his actions. Unconsciously he tested his mortality with a strategy of self-inflicted pain. Now he opts for the single goal of keeping safe.

Rehabilitation means claiming back the lost and forgotten inner child. His recovery requires him to reinstate autonomy and confidence, using the self-discipline so vital for emotional and spiritual well-being. It will take time for this guy's soul to resurface: he has carried out surgery on himself without anaesthetic. Suddenly he has been hurtled into the real world – a place where feelings are felt and expressed. All the programmes and treatment centres on offer have the same mission: to restore a sense of purpose to life.

And with it comes the recognition of what he has lost. That makes him angry: angry with himself and angry at the rest of the world. And the feeling just will not go away. He is the lion that weeps and the lion that roars.

Projecting too far into his future can be disastrous. If he is fearful that every day will be arduous, he won't be able to move forward. So he learns how to be gentle with himself and how to make a connection with people who share this affliction. In hearing other people's pain, he gets in touch with his own.

Transformation occurred when he embraced recovery, understanding enough to tend and heal his own wounds with the power of self-forgiveness. In time his soul opens up to the possibilities of interaction and sharing and he becomes considerate. When this happens, he has the potential to be an extraordinary human being.

 6/10   7/10

in real life

inconspicuous – he is the guy that says, 'No, thank you'.

the art of love

Any man who has been to hell and manages to redirect his life on the route back is worth his weight in gold. He has learnt how to disregard what no longer serves his purpose. Addiction has broken his heart, but he is still willing to love. He is in the early stages of self-discovery.

If you are attracted to a Recovering Addict, get the timing right. His addiction probably fostered abject loneliness and it is a painful process when the time comes to peel away the defensive layers, one by one. Not until he has resolved his anger about the past will he be able to handle a relationship in the present. Many situations in day-to-day life will act as triggers, pulling him back into his pain. It is crucial that he has built up the courage to deal with them without running away or looking to others for the solution.

This man will be a formidable task if he is involved with you for the wrong reasons.

You can see how ready he is for commitment by his approach to loving. If he is self-obsessed and thoughtless, then it is almost certain that he still fears the challenge of relationships.

Once he makes peace with himself, he will be able to relate to people free from the fear that they will be judgmental. This is an important milestone, a sign that he is beginning to learn how to love.

In honouring his human frailty and cowardice, he is transformed. He will be able to look back at his old life and wonder at how far he has come along the road. There is still a danger that the Recovering Addict may try too hard and overcompensate. He will be vulnerable so he needs to be validated and nurtured in a non-threatening way. But he welcomes the chance to explore being in love – something he does with care and caution.

 7/10   4/10

into action / interaction

the hook

Be prepared to be seduced, stalked or silenced – he is a multiple-choice kind of guy. Use your best judgment to gauge if he is willing to risk again: it's more than likely that he lost people on the way. Give him time and space. He will want to fall in love for real – just make sure you have a listening ear and a lot of patience. If you are a reactive personality, think before you speak.

into love

Keeping this relationship together will need a strong bond, open lines of communication and clear boundaries. Be available to him and his constant confessionals: he will want to share his progress with you. But allow time for yourself and your own feelings. He may want to avoid tricky situations but use tough love to reassure him.

out of love

You leaving him will be his worst nightmare: attempts to walk away spell rejection. He will want to fall to pieces. Whether he stands on his own two feet depends on how strong his belief in himself is. Do take time to reassure him. Don't feel guilty. If he's gone AWOL, watch your back.

love lesson
Acceptance is the answer.

performer

the archetype: The Magician, excitement seeker, plays to an audience, ego on wheels

the persona

how he appears to be

How to spot him – He holds himself well. He loves to observe and weigh up the competition. Flamboyant hand gestures, swanky dancing, hair flicks, pout and well-executed laughter all point to Mr Spotlight.

Dialogue / Verbal – One-liners taken from old black and white movies. He mimics his heroes, hoping to impress. He'll recite a sonnet or air guitar you after a measure or two. Great telephone manner.

Chat-line / Pick-up script – 'Will you be my leading lady?' 'I can help you with your demo tape.'

Life course – To be loved for his performance.

Accessories – Agent, Equity card, head-shots, show reel, demo tapes, ballet shoes, leggings, scripts, scores, stage make-up, family to fill the front row on first night.

Day job – Actor, dancer, mime artist, comedian, clown, singer, musician, presenter.

Babe history – Loads of. This talent may have been spoilt for choice. He knows when to turn the charm on, how much and who to. Admired from afar, he's clicked his heels to keep them entertained.

Theme song – 'Let Me Entertain You' by Robbie Williams.

Fantasy – Applause applause applause, giggle, moan, grunt, more applause applause, applause.

the shadow

who he really is

Bad habits – High anxiety, volatility. Window gazes anywhere he can see his reflection, seeks compliments, rehearses endlessly, flirts with his co-stars, rendered hysterical by bad press, sleeps late and runs out of milk.

What he doesn't say / Secrets and silences – 'Enough about me ... what do you think of me? I lied about my birthday. I'm star-struck.'

Hidden agenda – To find someone to make him famous for longer than fifteen minutes. To be stroppy and get away with it. To make people believe in him.

Philosophical mantra – I can't live without performing. It's in my blood.

Accessories – Rabbit's paw for luck, stage name, panic attacks, tissues, cheesy press clippings, collection of autographs, soap opera dependency, groupies, money tree.

Energy barometer – The more he works, the more he plays. He's usually an extrovert, making the most of his 'on' time.

Relationship future – He never knows where the road is going or if two can fit in his canoe.

Theme song – '... Baby One More Time' by Britney Spears.

Sex rating – He promises a lot but delivery rests on his ever-changing temperament. He's at ease with body-to-body contact so pull a fast one and take him unawares.

 3/10 5/10 6/10 6/10

aspects of the type

The Performer has purpose – he wants to be accomplished and inventive in whatever he does. He uses self-appraisal and constructive criticism to improve his expertise, fine tuning his skills. His perfectionist streak is revealed in his attention to detail. He may run every minute of his performance under the magnifying glass of self-criticism, ruthlessly focusing on details that others may not have even noticed.

As a Performer this guy is accustomed to rejection. But he is never comfortable with it when it happens. An unsuccessful audition or scathing criticism can really rock his confidence, sending him scurrying for refuge. When it all

path. Forget struggling in a bedsit: it may be where he started, but it sure won't be where he finishes! That fierce determination proves that the guy has the willpower to support his world of dreams. He believes in his talent. This belief in himself helps to keep him buoyant in the face of competition. And, after all, competition is the name of the game. He has to be courageous and tackle a variety of work to survive in the marketplace. Any work is better than no work.

The Performer type clearly loves the limelight. He would hate to fade into the background – undiscovered, unknown, alone. He believes that he has a gift: something that

He believes that he has a gift: something that other people will want to experience.

gets too much, he doses himself with past accolades and present flattery until faith is restored. Then he dusts himself off and gets out there again.

If he allows ambition to blind his creative vision, he will be relentless in the pursuit of fame and fortune. Nothing and no one will block his

other people will want to experience. Applause delights him. The opportunity to explore and express life experience through his chosen medium is of utmost importance. This is his life source: an inspiration which brings him huge contentment. Never still for a moment, he plans the next production, the next show, the next act.

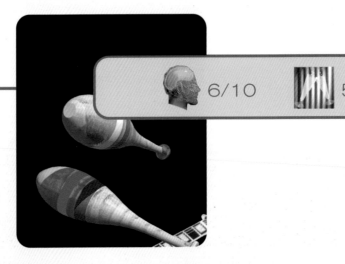

6/10   5/10

aspects of the soul

As a Performer this man must use his skills to communicate. He can become anyone he wishes. His gift for conceptualization is externalized in performance, and it is this that he transmits to his audience. When he delivers his piece, he hands over his vision, his enlightenment. He draws people into the world of his imagination, inviting them to believe that this is reality, if only for a moment. He plays directly to his audience's emotions. He may delight, disturb, disgust or mortify them, but whatever the emotion he is evocative. People respond to the disclosure they believe they are witnessing. To make this connection he must find a point of inner stillness. He must be centred and concentrated, and his spirit comes to life as he executes his magic.

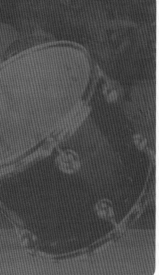

The work that the Performer undertakes allows him to adopt different personalities: masculine or feminine, strong or weak, happy or sad. If he is to be believable, he must be able to attune himself instinctively to the patterns of other people's lives. In this sense he is deeply empathetic. Yet, despite this inherent curiosity into what makes other people tick, he is essentially self-interested. The constant fear that his talent may dry up and disappear tortures him. But he does not disclose this to anyone.

He may be an escapist at heart, wishing to hide his real identity behind the mask of illusion. This type of guy does not reveal himself to just anyone. Oh, no. He will create an 'off-screen' persona, watching those he mixes with from behind a protective, neutral veneer. That way the real man, his true self, stays hidden. He is in touch with what is behind the persona, but the fear of being a phoney and of being found out is profound. He gives all that he is to his audience, but how much of that is the real him and how much is technique? This is why applause, recognition, is so important. Being a somebody in the eyes of others means that he is not a nobody to himself.

 6/10   4/10

in real life
the stripper, karaoke fan, busker, barrister

the art of love

What makes a great performer great? Sex appeal. There's an edge of sexuality in all this guy's uninhibited, irreverent displays of spontaneity. He may also play with comedy to lure you to him. He can certainly intoxicate you. But in love this guy is high maintenance. He wants to control how you see him. And, because he is famous in his own mind, there are stumbling blocks on the path to true love.

He looks for someone who will bolster his image: it doesn't hurt to have more attention drawn to him. Mind you, he would hate to be overshadowed by a newcomer. Especially his newcomer.

He puts his whole heart into everything he does and that includes his love life. This guy is accustomed to working with heightened emotion: he frequently experiences adrenaline rushes and increased heart rate in his professional life so he searches for this same buzz, this intensity, in love. He may zoom around with many a pretty face but his commitment he saves for last. His off-screen persona, worn for the public eye, hides the longing for a kindred spirit. He needs to share his complexity, his fear, his weakness with another human being.

This may not be so easy. Not everyone is willing to take a Performer on board. His insecurities can cause him to become anxious, even paranoid. He gets a high from his work but can fall from great heights in a second. His reputation and off-screen persona are forefront in his mind when he is social. He is not always sure when he can relax into a more subdued self. In love the Performer is a chameleon. He can sense what women are looking for in a man. But he is so adept and so confident in his ability to produce emotion that he may automatically dismiss his feelings as inauthentic. This type does not turn inward as much as would be good for him. He has to have time and space to move from his off-screen persona to his private self.

♥ 7/10　　👁 6/10

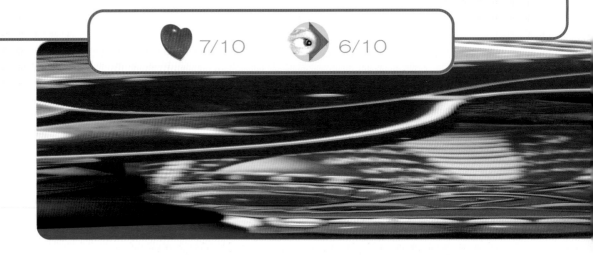

into action / interaction

the hook

Be audacious but not too headstrong. Send him flowers on opening night. Blow him kisses from the wings. Throw him your knickers. Ask for his autograph. Tell him repeatedly how much you love his work. Discuss common idols. Volunteer to start the fan club. Offer to protect him from groupies. But maintain your equality all the while. You do this by smiling. Seduce him with your wantonness: pretend that you're only after one thing.

into love

Love him for what he is, not for his achievements. Appreciate his winning formula in taste and style. Help him to abandon the romantic-lover script he has absorbed through music, dance and cinema. Bring him into reality by challenging his sense of self. Is he feeling what you are feeling? Encourage him to 'be' feelings instead of 'do' feelings. If he takes your lead, this will bring him personal satisfaction as he grows closer to you and to himself.

out of love

Take it gently. He is easily hurt because of his fear of rejection and of being found out. Continue to run the fan club.

love lesson

Adore him but don't be the understudy. Make sure that he doesn't shut you out of his world.

cyber man

the archetype: The Magician, manic web wiz, extra-terrestrial trekker, travels the virtual world

the persona

how he appears to be

How to spot him – Cruising the websites. He hangs in the chat room, is chained to his laptop in the office and on public transport. He surfs the bottom shelf at the newsagent.

Dialogue / Verbal – Monosyllabic. He's quiet as a mouse: 'Gotta go now – it's chat-line time'. Doesn't volunteer information but loves to get nutty about his latest viewing.

Chat-line / Pick-up script – 'Are you a dot com?' 'I can tailor-make you a site if you like.' 'What colour knickers are you wearing?'

Life course – To browse alternative realities in cyberspace.

Accessories – Coffee mugs, computer, scanner, floppy discs, tape cartridges, Zip drives, anti-virus programmes, well-thumbed 1,000-page user's manual, digital camera, halogen lamp, ergonomic furniture, doctors for back, eye and neck complaints.

Day job – Computer technician or salesman, website designer, software supplier, desk-top publisher, computer scientist, communication systems employee, applications programmer.

Babe history – Me, myself and my modem.

Theme song – 'Are "Friends" Electric' by Gary Numan.

Fantasy – To enter the twilight zone: a computer-generated environment where he has close encounters with beatific strangers.

the shadow

who he really is

Bad habits – Stays too long at the shrine, runs up huge phone bills, forgets to water the plants and has night sweats. Falls asleep at dinner, has too few real-life friends and is unfit.

What he doesn't say / Secrets and silences – 'I can't come now .... I'm having cyber sex. I am part of the techno-warrior community. I'm connected and you're not. I'm anonymous.'

Hidden agenda – To seek out the dark places of cyberspace for on-line pleasure. To surf all day long.

Philosophical mantra – Technology is the future.

Accessories – Coffee stains on his bathrobe, hungry fish, overflowing ashtray, estranged parents, sci-fi novels, computer dictionary, state-of-the-art tech toys, hard-drive archive.

Energy barometer – Low physical energy but high left-hemisphere activity. He's not as flexible as he used to be.

Relationship future – If he can give up the secret cyber babes, he may have a chance of getting together with an earthling.

Theme song – 'Hyperballad' by Björk.

Sex rating – Low, unless there's dirty, on-line chatback. Sexuality is saved for http://www.what's your preference.com.

 9/10   3/10   4/10   7/10

aspects of the type

When Cyber Man hangs the 'Do Not Disturb' sign on the door and logs on, he forgets real life as he knows it and boards his own Starship Enterprise. Fibre optics help him make the quantum leap from his place to home page. His brain cells ping pong into play as he enters new terrain. Time and distance dissolve. His hand

had to trudge through compu-jargon to make sense of his reality. Breaking down this new language was his initiation. To learn more about the possibilities of artificial intelligence he has become incredibly analytical. He is part of a huge, worldwide community where all are welcome, thriving on the processes of accessing and manipulating information at

He has a nifty knack of making connections, parallel or plural.

guides his imagination as he whirls through the configurations of instant intelligence. It is information he craves. He scans the screen, downloading anything that grabs him. He has a nifty knack of making connections, parallel or plural. This virtual world has no boundaries, no locked doors. Life on Mars is now a possibility.

The hard-core type literally lives at his computer. He is self-taught. He may have been a loner at school, who redirected his social time to keyboard time, or a high achiever, who was sidelined because of his nerdish behaviour. He is defined by his skills. Being a cyber guy, he has

will. If he is a technical wizard, he uses his expertise to simulate his own thinking with creative, problem-solving programmes that combine logic, mathematics and graphic skills.

He believes wholeheartedly that high tech is here to stay. The Cyber Man's reality is simple. He can be anywhere he wants to be at any time. He feels part of a growing sub-culture that supports him as he sits at his desk and wastes his lunch hour in the chat room. He plugs in to avoid loneliness or boredom, or both. Too much time spent at the terminal can make his personality hard to fathom.

 5/10 2/10

aspects of the soul

Cyber Man has a very clear understanding of who he is. His soul may not be obvious, but it is there. He has a deep-rooted conviction that it is the method of disseminating information that shapes society. He is dedicated to a fresh beginning with a more democratic conduit for meaning that offers participation and interaction to us all. The confines of the real word – the borders, the institutions, the rules and regulations, the silent conditioning that penetrates every one of us – are challenged by this type. History starts again here.

In communication he is inclined towards the minimal, eliminating anything that is superfluous. The aesthetics of computer language, like those of mathematics, lie in the simplicity and truth of its logic. The elegant solution to a problem has a mystical dimension for him. This is his illumination, his way of breaking through the monotony of everyday life.

Cyberspace is the repository of all kinds of fascinations from ninja index launchpads to monumental 3D experiments. In real life this guy is a face in the crowd but here he can perfect his fantasies. He travels the electronic frontier to find a place where he belongs. The cyber punk imbued with special powers, the sci-fi android and the prince of peace – all are figures in a reality he accesses through his computer, and all assume the role of the mythical hero, which is to save the world. As the matrix of imaginations interconnect, Cyber Man re-invents himself at will. This is key to the guy's need to return again and again to the screen. We have always been alone in the landscape of the imagination but now cyberspace allows imaginary worlds to be shared and experienced by anyone. For Cyber Man it is a spiritual experience. And for him soul searching extends into the jungle of cyber conspiracy theory with its discourse on who or what has ultimate power.

 2/10   4/10

in real life

the late-night office worker, bored house-mate, unemployed graduate, isolated teenager, sexual deviant

the art of love

On-line this guy is anonymous. He is who he wants to be, depending on his mood. He can be gay or bisexual, married or single, rich or poor, tall or short. He can even be a woman if he wants to find out more about the opposite sex.

The intensity of cyber courtship comes from the apparent directness of the encounter know how to interact with a partner on a physical level – perhaps he feels love but is unable to express it without a keyboard. Or maybe he is attracted to the convenience of anonymity – just dabbling for a quick fix. After all, if he goes on line and plays with words well enough he can get a fabulous response. He can

and the lack of normal distractions. Dialogue between Cyber Man and his on-line babe builds to intimate exchanges far faster than in real life. Close encounters of the computer kind are unpunctuated. There are no 'ums' or 'aahs', no pauses or interruptions. Cyber Man is not a physical presence; he is a virtual presence. The zone of interaction is minimized and the conversation selective. Essentially, he gives only to receive back.

There may be no restrictions on fantasy, but this guy must keep his on-line personality in check if he is to hold his two worlds in separate compartments. So what's the draw? He may not gorge his ego like a hungry lion at the kill. He feels so loved, so sought after, so 'one in a million'. And this is the danger. Love on the internet is nothing like love in the real world. He doesn't have to deal with the annoying habits and mannerisms that drive real couples crazy. He doesn't have to wake up next to her or clean up after her. He convinces himself that love hassle-free is better than true love, which lies in that midheaven between the sacred and the profane. Compared to the level of his intellectual interaction, his emotional integrity is limited. Never mind. He's happy to do it all again tomorrow.

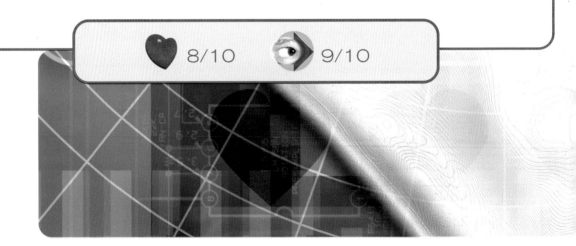

♥ 8/10   9/10

into action / interaction

the hook

Enter the twilight zone. Your password is the golden key. Punch in: *is anybody out there?* Await reply.

D.L.I.A.D.T.
Library

into love

Be his romantic power point. Juggle two worlds. Use your judgment: don't enter restricted areas.

out of love

Wish him well. Disconnect politely. Then hit the escape button.

love lesson

Download him from the virtual to the real. Activate his interpersonal skills by drawing him into the world.

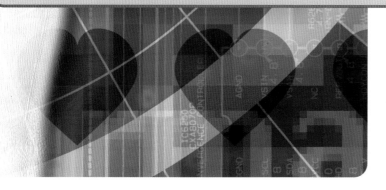

dictator

the archetype: The King, high-profile warrior, power junkie, charismatic and autocratic

the persona

how he appears to be

How to spot him – In public and behind the scenes, the performance is consistent – he demands centre stage. He's the one cracking the jokes in a circle of friends. He laughs as loud as he shouts.

Dialogue / Verbal – Sophisticated. Everything is well planned, scripted and rehearsed: no slips of the tongue for this guy. He has off-the-scale charisma, and his silver tongue and deep voice make women melt.

Chat-line / Pick-up script – 'Kiss me or I'll kill you.'

Life course – Global domination.

Accessories – Million-dollar shark smile, immaculate filing system, fresh underwear every day, hand-written 'to do' lists, cash in back pocket, toe-nail clipper, gold chain, state-of-the-art wristwatch, daily agenda.

Day job – Headmaster, team manager, military general, drug baron, boss of international criminal organization, sweat-shop mogul.

Babe history – Directing the female players in a 'Dungeons and Dragons' scenario. Escape and seek wise counsel from those that went before.

Theme song – 'My Favourite Game' by The Cardigans.

Fantasy – Special category in the mile-high club: oral foreplay from a nameless nymphet, handcuffed to avoid ejection during turbulence.

the shadow

who he really is

Bad habits – Pompous, dogmatic. Spends no time planning things for you to do together, buys your affection and is never alone.

What he doesn't say / Secrets and silences – 'I want to be cloned. When I first started out, I wanted to save the world. Never compare me to another man.

Hidden agenda – To target power-crazed women. To block the horrors of his life with escapist daydreams.

Philosophical mantra – I'm going to live forever.

Accessories – Hit list, pasta cookbook, headache cures, late-night videos, stress-release grip balls, hair dye, supply of apology gifts.

Energy barometer – Mental activity: 24 hours a day. Physical activity: combination of lazy and hyper-active, depleted by high anxiety levels. Catch him on the up and he'll dazzle you with his performance.

Relationship future – There isn't one unless you opt for surrendering your two pennies' worth – submission and discretion will be the ultimate requirements. Unconquered geishas cause occasional flutters of the heart.

Theme song – 'It's A Man's, Man's, Man's World' by James Brown.

Sex rating – Mostly wham-bam-thank-you-ma'am. He pumps up the volume the nearer that he gets to demi-god status.

 4/10 3/10 5/10 10/10

aspects of the type

A textbook example of megalomania, the Dictator is characterized as enslaved by a craving for wealth, grandeur and power. Power corrupts so he may be an idealist who has gone off the rails. Spiralling downwards, he may have chosen to ignore his conscience, dismissing it as irrelevant.

His world is self-created and he is driven by an insatiable ambition to enforce his own ethics. They are key to how he sees himself and how he wants others to see him. 'Highly

Vicious and malicious, he'll take your skin off and hand it back to you with a smile on his face. But by choice he operates from a distance rather than close up. When he can, he'll leave others to do the dirty work, and he avoids the consequences of his actions by walking away, cutting off from his feelings. A real give-away in social situations is the hollow laugh with the chilly undertone. All part of the

> ## Hand in hand with the Dictator's need to dominate is an instinctive lack of trust in others.

disciplined' and 'ritualistic' best describe this guy, and he needs to feel respected by his community. But in truth the rules are created for others to follow – he makes them and then breaks them.

Hand in hand with the Dictator's need to dominate is an instinctive lack of trust in others. Delusions of grandeur and persecution do battle inside his head and obedience becomes all important. With the paranoid fear of losing control flooding his thoughts, his powers of manipulation become pivotal in the maintenance of his ideology. To satisfy his urge for iconic status, he'll charm you to the nth degree if he wants you. Equally, he won't hesitate to resort to hard-core control to enforce his will. Nothing is accidental; everything is premeditated.

package, it is designed to make any audience feel inferior.

There are few likeable qualities in this guy. His passion for self-protection wipes out any possibility of sentiment. Sensitivity to others' thoughts and feelings is not valued. He will view this as weakness – an indication of loss of control, something he cannot bear to have happen to others, let alone himself. Ironically, it is Dr Evil's inability to control himself that destroys him.

If he could, the Dictator would mainline power, and perversely that's what anyone drawn to him wants too. Power is glamorous, but even if you are hooked on a challenge, think again, and again, and again, *and* again. Unless, of course, submission comes easily to you.

 4/10   8/10

aspects of the soul

The doorway to his soul is locked and bolted, and only he holds the key. Fuelled by charm and rage, he has switched sensitivity for supremacy and in doing so he repeatedly denies his spirit.

Charisma is his calling card and he uses it unscrupulously. Those on the receiving end, his peons, are made to feel simultaneously elevated and worthless. They are momentarily part of a magic that he conjures up to win them over to accept that his purpose is *their* purpose. He knows how flattering it is to be drawn into the charmed circle – you feel dazzled and special – and so he distracts and disarms people to dominate them. The flip side is his terrifying capacity for rage. Look out if he's in danger of losing face. This triggers self-protection and the eruption will be Vesuvian. It is the potent combination of rage and charm that makes a Dictator so invincible and others so malleable: the man can do anything.

But it is also the source of his isolation. Detachment keeps the Dictator distanced from those he may truly care for and eventually the absence of closeness is internalized. This happens when he has emotionally and spiritually abandoned all intimacy and sensitivity. There is no one home, and, as a consequence, any hope of peace of mind is lost. It is a painful place at which to arrive.

For the Dictator, spirituality is replaced with an extreme dogma which may be religious. It's what justifies his actions and it's the way he attempts to stifle his fears of loss of control. But there are two things which no one can control: the first is love and the second is death. Love is unconfinable and death is unpredictable. He is more frightened by death than anything else, and that springs from a lifetime's avoidance of pain and of the consequences of his actions. A Dictator's recurring nightmare is judgment, which will be personified in the father figure of God whether he be religious or not. He constantly reassures himself with a kind of false immortality – by magnifying his own power and importance in the here and now.

 1/10   2/10

in real life

the domineering boyfriend, aggressive company boss, dysfunctional father, power-crazy official

the art of love

The temptation to be extraordinary is overwhelming for the Dictator. He likes to promote himself as a larger-than-life character. Being ordinary and in tune with the rest of the world is too scary for him. He must avoid being victimized. He needs to win and he wins by being invincible.

Does he want to love? The answer is probably yes, but he has no idea how because he has never been taught. Or never learnt. At some stage in his life this man made a conscious decision not to get hurt. Indications are that this type is closely associated with attempts to avoid re-living some intensely painful childhood experience. Certainly anger is a manifestation of psychological pain – specifically feelings of hurt, guilt, shame and failure – and he chooses to externalize his pain in direct confrontation, through fits of red-hot rage.

To prevent the possibility of further trauma, he sacrifices spontaneous love for a repressed substitute for love, which is distorted and coloured by his habit of persecution. So, believing that obedience is the ultimate sign of love, he seeks submissiveness in any partner.

In effect, his masculinity is rooted in a pattern of domination which disempowers others. To reinforce his authority, he becomes ever more dominant and judgmental.

But his self-image is dire. He is cut off from all intimacy. His temper is compulsive. Forgiveness is never the first option. He must punish. Yet the ferocity of his emotion terrifies him. The toxic overflow decimates any possibility of love. And this loss of control results in a huge sense of inadequacy.

Inevitably, love is a series of disappointments. His downfall will be his inability to see the real person. He projects his own needs and fears onto any woman he is attracted to, picturing her as the Madonna, completely pure and to be adored from afar, or as the Whore, for whom he feels nothing but contempt. She, in turn, may be magnetized by his charisma, but frightened when he blows a circuit. Can he win her over? How successful he is at making up will always mean more to her than to him. Self-transformation through the integration of his sensitivity would be incredibly liberating for this type.

 3/10   4/10

into action / interaction

the hook

You'll find him on the dark side of the moon. If you enjoy being under this guy's influence, lower your head when he speaks to you and agree when he insults you. Be prepared to take dictation.

into love

Have a lobotomy.

out of love

Raise your own tolerance threshold.

love lesson

Work on diffusing confrontation. You're never going to come out on top.

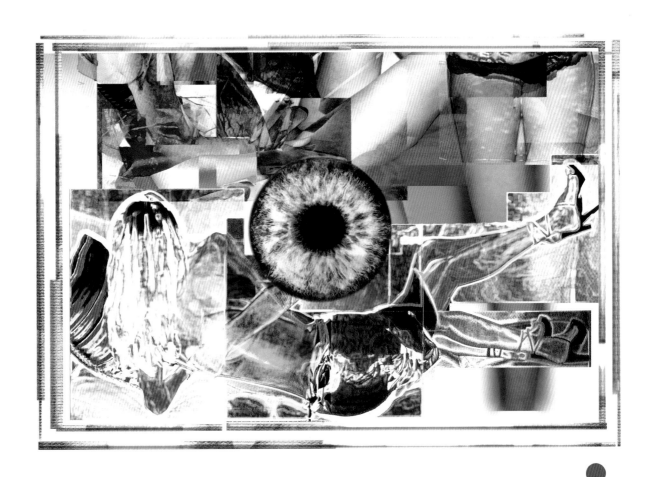

artist

the archetype: The Lover, creator, aesthetic innovator, experimental and conceptual

the persona

how he appears to be

How to spot him – With the freak set. Find him beside his recent work, looking nervous or resplendent. He's self-styled and happy with it. His look is never forced. Whatever the genre, he shines.

Dialogue / Verbal – Articulate and exuberant, inquisitive and cultured, voluble and volatile, he oozes creativity.

Chat-line / Pick-up script – 'I'd be interested to know what you think of my work. Does it speak to you?' 'Quite frankly, you're surreal and I'd like to capture it.' 'Mine's an open studio.'

Life course – To remain gifted.

Accessories – Metal, wood, plastic, bronze, clay, marble, paint, papier-mâché, film/video camera, easel, chaise longue, screen, darkroom, pen and ink, typewriter, dictaphone, dealer list.

Day job – Visual artist in any medium, writer, poet.

Babe history – On couch, in mould, on film, on paper: all have played their part in the creative process, and there's a twinkle in his eye when he remembers them.

Theme song – 'Tangled Up In Blue' by Bob Dylan.

Fantasy – The realm of the senses: *ménage à trois* with current muse and ex-muse, their identities are concealed. Nirvana.

the shadow

who he really is

Bad habits – Mood swings extraordinaire: he cries with joy and spontaneously combusts with fury. He is self-obsessed and needs constant attention. He locks himself away in his work space and doesn't mutter a word for days if things aren't going to plan.

What he doesn't say / Secrets and silences – 'I haven't got one roving eye ... I've got two. When the work's finished, so are we. Do me a favour and leave me alone. I need flattery for breakfast, lunch and dinner. Sponsor me, why don't you?'

Hidden agenda – To leave a lasting impression. To provoke. To be recognized by the Establishment. To screw the Establishment.

Philosophical mantra – Expression is the unveiling of truth.

Accessories – Unopened bills, fish-and-chip habit, stale wine, hard cheese, squat mates, overdraft, scruffy mad dog, paint-strewn outfits, hat collection, antique cigarette holder, self-portrait in shreds.

Energy barometer – High low, high low.

Relationship future – It's a blank canvas, baby.

Theme song – 'Night Nurse' by Gregory Isaacs.

Sex rating – Great at seduction. He likes to create an intense atmoshere to get it on.

 5/10 4/10 8/10 5/10

aspects of the type

For the Artist, work is play. He is true to the inner voice which demands that he express himself, and, with passion as his life force, he has the spontaneity to be creative. Through his vision, existence is more fully explored. Steadfast in his dedication to his art form as he strives to get his message across, he is a romantic figure, absorbed in emotion, beauty and concept.

a missing link in a bountiful universe – and so he creates a bubble in which he can cut himself off from ordinary existence. This type will give up everything to do what he has to do. His purpose is to prove his authenticity, not to anyone else, but to himself. He gives his art his all and in the midst of a new creation he may lock himself away and work like a man possessed.

He is a romantic figure, absorbed in emotion, beauty and concept.

This man is profoundly sensitive to every aspect of his environment and he relies heavily on the stimulus he draws from it. Often he is drawn to the sensual, to the bizarre, to the extreme. As the raw material of his dreams and visions, his perceptions are filtered through the web of his imagination to create new meaning. He may have a provocative, avant-garde approach to his art or be a traditionalist. Moments of inspiration make him dizzy with joy as he is rocketed to another dimension in his eagerness to convey what he feels about a certain person, a certain situation, a certain attitude.

This guy is inclined to be contemplative and aloof. Life is art, he believes, and there is a certain disdain for what is commonplace or unimaginative. He thinks of himself as chosen –

Because his work is a central part of his personality, this type needs constant bolstering. He must feel that he is accepted by his circle. Approval and recognition are essential for his self-esteem – they validate his contribution to the world and that is important to him. If you fancy an Artist type, beware the frail ego. Unfortunately, he is incredibly sensitive to negative criticism. He is so attached to his work that he won't be capable of taking it lightly – everything is taken personally. How he chooses to respond will give you a real sense of his inner personality.

Check his work out before you attempt to make contact with him on a romantic level. He won't be that interested if you are not overly enthusiastic about what he does.

6/10   5/10

aspects of the soul

The Artist's soul is laid bare at every stage of every piece of work he produces. Each time his aim is to make a personal statement about a particular issue. This may be concealed, due to the nature of the work, but the intention is there and his objective is always to elicit a fresh response. It is his interpretation of what he sees, hears, feels, touches and tastes that gives life to his aesthetic as he moves through the processes of contemplation, realization and internal criticism.

He will be conscious of the long shadow that religion has cast on the history and development of creative expression. But he has his own faith. To find and express his truth is his ultimate. The void of emptiness, of nothingness, does not perplex this type. He fills the space with words or images to create his own interpretation of existence. And in this way, as he pushes the boundaries of self-expression, he takes on the role of co-creator or mediator.

Whether he is hedonistic and vulgar or shy and gentle, the Artist is in tune with his energies. He lives within his creative unconscious and picks up on its sensations and vibrations, open to invasion from the zone of the collective unconscious. His heightened awareness and intuition allow even his most abstract ideas to come to fruition. His acute sensitivity tunes him into the poignancy and the subtlety of many areas of life. Affected by everything that goes on around him, whether it be magnificence or atrocity, he feels free to express his responses. And this freedom is his ticket to being at one with himself. Intellect and emotion unite as he speaks through a personal language of symbol or sign.

Giving birth to ideas and seeing them take shape before his eyes thrills him and brings a sense of satisfaction. It's what keeps him alive and happy to be mortal. So when the work is going well, his euphoria makes him great to be around. But his soul is also the place that houses his deepest fears, and he will struggle with the demons of self-doubt when his talent is not recognized or acknowledged. Life, for him, is like a revolving door, as he experiences the highs and lows of the artistic psyche.

 5/10   4/10

in real life

the amateur artist, unpublished writer, pamphlet poet, home-made card giver, home-video junkie, ice sculptor, origami maker

the art of love

The Artist welcomes the esctasy of love with open arms. His sensuality requires that he draw you in: into his mind, into his heart and into his body. Love for this guy can be enchanting and all-consuming. He'll want to leap into a relationship if he gets the green light, sweeping you off your feet as he kidnaps your heart, whispering sweet nothings and taking you to heaven and back. He loves longingly, and his heart beats faster when the object of his desire moves into his orbit. His fantasies are realized in a fast-flowing Technicolor river of passion and arousal.

The unfolding of love is very precious to him and he will try to establish truth within a relationship. He may not always want to articulate his feelings, but, when he does, they will be beautifully expressed. He is a very considerate type and his disposition can often be exploited. His desire to please will be shown in the way he gives gifts that have a sentimental quality. He brings a softness to love that could last forever. And if his partner possesses a gentle attitude towards loving, it will certainly bring out his warm and fuzzy side. Any partner will have to nourish his artistic temperament and whoever

he attracts must be his and his alone. But the ties he has with other women are important to him too and may even represent an aspect of his work. Don't even think about attempting to sever them.

The muse who catches his eye and heart will need to tread carefully. This type is no stranger to the dark side of love. He is overtly sensitive and may want to hold onto a beautiful moment for too long. He can sometimes lose perspective and become insecure, possessive, defensive, even suffocating. Because he finds it difficult to diffuse negative feelings he cannot recognize the impact such behaviour may have on his partner. It is important for him to make sense of another person's need for space.

Certainly he is a feeler, a type that wants to experience love at its most sublime, and he hates to consider failure. He may keep unrealistic expectations of love in place to deny the fact that most relationships begin with hope and end in pain. What is clear is that he surrenders to love. What he has to learn is that love has a natural cycle of its own. Like the vine, sometimes it dies and sometimes it flourishes.

♥ 9/10   👁 7/10

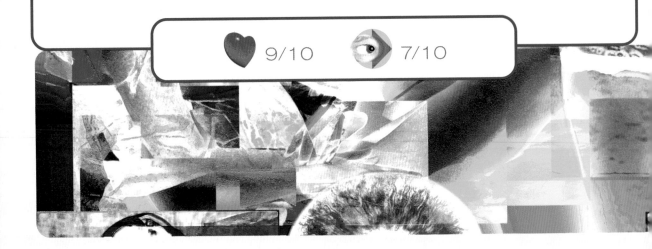

into action / interaction

the hook

Wear a mask, veil your identity and let his fantasies multiply. You must be a goddess or a witch – different for sure. He loves the mystical, magical power of a woman. Be his inspiration, always staying just a step away from his grasp. Move like the swaying grass in the wind and you will not fail to catch his eye. Be confident in your womanliness and lure him with your 'out-of-bounds' tactics.

into love

You can't afford to fool with his heart: it's fragile. This type needs to be reminded that he's important to you, but stay away from co-dependent behaviour. Fit around his schedule, which will undoubtedly be chaotic. Bring love into the confines of reality by waking him out of the dream and encouraging him to address his naïvety. He's hot-wired for desire so keep his eye from wandering by maintaining the mystery of your love.

out of love

Insecurity meltdowns may leave you mopping him up all too often. Is he worth it? If he puts too much pressure on the relationship by being possessive and jealous, leave with a fleeting goodbye.

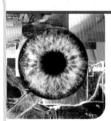

love lesson

Express your wildest dreams but be sure not to lose sight of what's real and what's not.

eco warrior

the archetype: The Warrior, visionary, intuitive creator, cyclical celebrant

the persona

how he appears to be

How to spot him – Starstruck on a moonlit night. Clock the boots; then the clothes (earth colours) and the face (weathered features separate him from the pretty boys as he stands tall in his masculinity).

Dialogue / Verbal – Green-speak, maybe regional accent, a spade-is-a-spade, no-frills kinda guy. Dislikes noise pollution of any kind.

Chat-line / Pick-up script – 'Don't panic. It's organic.' 'You ride a bicycle – how fantastic!' 'I never buy flowers. I grow them myself.' 'Are you anti-nuclear …?'

Life course – To realize his own potential by setting up self-sustaining eco-structures.

Accessories – Axe, secateurs and shovel, wheelbarrow and organic farmyard manure, hose, weather vane, mountain bike, tent, foul-weather gear, open fire-place.

Day job – Gardener, gamekeeper, forester, fisherman, eco-activist, marine biologist, horticulturist, farmer, bee-keeper, geologist, tree-surgeon.

Babe history – One-woman man who's been disappointed in the past. Searching for a companion prepared to go off the beaten track.

Theme song – 'Harvest Moon' by Neil Young.

Fantasy – Oberon with his doting Titania, hidden from view in the dense woods: a midsummer night's dream.

the shadow

who he really is

Bad habits – His eco-ego makes him a poor listener on subjects he claims as his. Eats roots and leaves, finds it difficult to share a task and enjoys wearing smelly socks.

What he doesn't say / Secrets and silences – 'I want to be alone when I'm doing my own thing. Are you happy in the kitchen? No, you can't come fishing. Boys do cry.'

Hidden agenda – To meet and mate mature Girl Guide for outdoor ventures and picnics.

Philosophical mantra – Me Tarzan. You Jane.

Accessories – Noose and whip, cow prod, drinking buddies, damsels in distress.

Energy barometer – From sun up to sun down.

Relationship future – Feet on the ground, head in the clouds.

Theme song – 'King of Pain' by The Police.

Sex rating – Hang on to your hat. He's orgasmic! Get ready for outdoor escapes and sex in the sun, wind, rain and snow.

 7/10 7/10 9/10 5/10

aspects of the type

Central to the Eco Warrior's personality is his mystery. He's a dark horse, and dark horses are always intriguing. That intrigue combined with charm make this type one of the most seductive there is. If you manage to engage him in conversation, he'll be off and running with topics that inspire him. He is a philosopher of a kind: he'll build a house and discuss the building of it with you. It's the nature of him – how he defines himself and his narrative – that holds the attention. This man is complex and cool.

in the reality of our lives on this planet. Any disillusion in his daily life is counterbalanced by his response to the cycle of the seasons. From dark to light, winter to spring and from scarcity to abundance, they bring balance and harmony to what, he recognizes, would otherwise be a harsh existence. His daily meditation is a connection with the earth. The sense of solitude that he feels encourages one of his most endearing qualities: the desire to nurture. As a practical visionary, he sees what is possible and kick-starts whatever resources are needed to achieve his objective.

> **Solitude ... encourages one of his most endearing qualities: the desire to nurture.**

He is not necessarily a team player. Many Eco Warriors choose solo professions. This is because most of all he loves to be alone, relishing his own space and time. Whether in the forest, on top of a mountain, sleeping under the stars or sweating under the sun, the natural environment is his playground. He smells the roses he grows but where does the fragrance take him? No one knows.

He may deny aspects of his personality in a bid to stay silent and 'safe', yet he is grounded

He is a survivor. His eco-politics provide a belief structure which empowers a need to make his mark on the world. The sustaining of projects that enhance the quality of life in the community is of prime importance to him – you'll find him planting trees where there were none, encouraging our natural surroundings to flourish. He is a testament to longevity and legacy. This is a man who cares about the past, the present and the future of this planet.

6/10   5/10

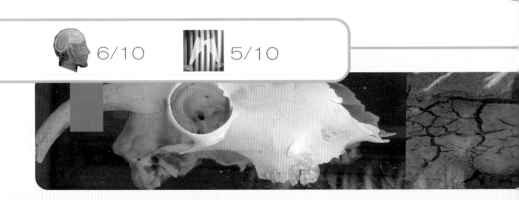

aspects of the soul

Here is a man who spends much of his time outdoors in the fresh air. He loves to build fires, to chop wood and dig. In this respect he enjoys many of the simple pleasures of our caveman ancestors. Happy inside his own skin, his masculine side is fulfilled. This makes him incredibly attractive to others, who see him as self-sufficient. He embraces sensuality: he loves to feel the dust and dirt in the palm of his hand. It is through his physicality that he constructs his external world and uniquely he recognizes and celebrates that awareness.

He is not a superficial man. He has learnt to confront fear by accepting the forces of nature. His dream is to honour his commitment to the earth, and this unconquerable impulse feeds his internal strength.

But the Eco Warrior is wrapped up in his own world. Although his affinity with his natural environment allows him to contemplate in solitude the essence of who he is and what he wants from his life, both with and away from other people, his insular personality casts a shadow on his soul. This is because his connection with the physical environment is his ultimate connection. It is more natural, more instinctive, than the link between him and his chosen partner. He may even avoid closeness. Trapped by his desire to explore his primal roots, his perception of reality may be distorted so that he sees himself as a loner and he rarely believes that he has what he deserves in a relationship.

Emotionally you may have to stick it out with this one. Often unable to volunteer his feelings, he creates a barrier between the world and himself, retreating into nature where, it seems, he is totally accepted, totally welcomed and totally absorbed by the search for peace and inner harmony. He will appear enigmatic, but that's only natural for a man who doesn't let you know what he most wants and needs. Deep grief can often be manifest as arrogance. Beware him returning to his habitat. The outdoor world provides him with a safe haven of sacred places where he can contemplate from afar. Make sure he takes you with him.

 6/10 8/10

in real life

the compost maker, re-cycler, bird rescuer, Greenpeace member, hemp-shoe wearer, cyclist, tepee maker

the art of love

In love the Eco Warrior may realize his dreams but never invite others to share them. This is because he finds it difficult to be inclusive. It is not because he doesn't want to; it is because he doesn't know how.

Secrecy and alienation are second nature to him when he finds himself in a social situation where he is not entirely at ease. In many ways he comes across as unfriendly and cold. But this stems from his sense of pride. Superiority may veil his true vulnerability. Remember that it is only a façade.

He realizes a mature masculine identity through his vitality and by being in touch with his own physicality. In many ways he is an almost mythical figure. His romantic imagination frames a sequence of expressive sexual images. This guy is ritualistic, and his sensuality will surprise, delight and excite anyone invited into such intimate moments.

As a provider, he can be overpowering and dominant without meaning to be. For many Eco Warrior types this is an automatic defence tactic. He is demonstrating a need to keep everything together and in control. If he senses a loss of control, he will feel threatened. Sadly this lack of consideration can drive others away.

Yet the Eco Warrior wants to share common values in partnership. Before he makes a choice in love matters, he will test you by exploring interests, opinions and attitudes. His expectations are high because he is faithful, steadfast and good-hearted. In love the Eco Warrior has patience. Sexual compatibility will be as important to him as naturalness. He will value you beyond his own personal gain.

♥ 8/10   ◉ 4/10

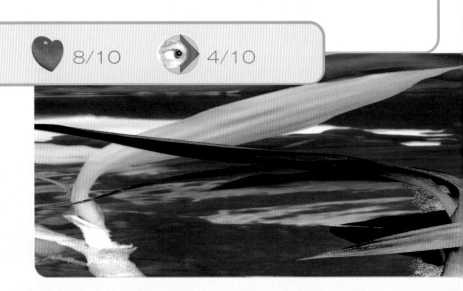

into action / interaction

the hook

Recite after me, 'I support Save the Whale, I dance with wolves and I don't drop litter'. Connect with him on an ethical level; then bring your femininity to bear. He doesn't like lipstick (ugh, it tastes horrible) and he doesn't like perfume (it camouflages your scent). Physically, this guy wants the real you. The more real you are, the more raunchy, the more ravenous he becomes. If you want him, a subtle seduction is best. Simplicity is beautiful to the Eco Warrior. *Au naturel* is a real turn-on, but if you're not, don't try faking it.

into love

Love with this type has potential. Side by side is where he wants to be – in trust, in truth and in openness – but he has demons of his own that will harm the relationship. Let him fight the good fight. Encourage his journey into himself by not being reactive when it is his own soul he is confronting. Bring tenderness, innocence and consistency into his life. Gather food from the fields and prepare it together. Wealth to the Eco Warrior is a sophisticated balance between what is necessary and what is available.

out of love

If you want to run, cover your trail well. This guy will track you. You can't hide. It will be a struggle to stay away when he calls you back to him. An exposed or concealed sensitivity makes him an exception to the rule where break-ups are concerned: he finds it difficult to say goodbye. 'Let's be friends – let's remain lovers and on my terms' would be an ideal solution for him. He relishes his isolation but is scared of abandonment. If you really want out, book yourself into another time zone.

love lesson

Remind him that love is the most powerful force in the universe.

obsessive lover

the archetype: The Lover, damaged romantic, clinging ex, ostrich with his head in the sand

the persona

how he appears to be

How to spot him – He's full of life and enthusiasm if he is in love, forlorn and sad if he is between emotional fixes. Harangues the DJ to play love songs. Can't take his eyes off you if you gave him the push.

Dialogue / Verbal – Smooth-talking charmer. Complimentary, nervous, quick to arrange a rendezvous. His objective is to entice you into being with him so he'll look for similarities to make connections.

Chat-line / Pick-up script – 'Did we meet or was it all a dream?' 'You know you can't resist me so give in now.' 'We're destined to be together, if you'd only see it.'

Life course – To find his 'other half'.

Accessories – Florist account, champagne corks, love mementos, framed photos, compilation love songs, bath-time love potions, heart-shaped pin-board, spare fluffy bathrobe, rubber ducky, Velcro to attach his heart to yours.

Day job – Anything, but he likes his evenings free so he can go out on the rebound.

Babe history – Plays emotional rubber-banding with all the girls he has ever loved. He can never say goodbye.

Theme song – 'Love Is The Drug' by Roxy Music.

Fantasy – The Garden of Eden before the Fall: Adam and Eve get on a treat.

the shadow

who he really is

Bad habits – Won't accept that 'over' means 'over and out', leaves messages on ex-lover's answering machine and/or bombards his victim with e-mails, finds excuses to drop by and stays in touch with his ex-lover's friends and family.

What he doesn't say / Secrets and silences – 'I'm going to make you love me.'

Hidden agenda – To be loved in spite of who he is.

Philosophical mantra – Love is forever.

Accessories – Restraining order, relationship therapist, anti-depressants, bored friends, 'return to sender' mail, returned engagement rings, well-thumbed co-dependent self-help books.

Energy barometer – All his emotional energy goes into dreaming, peaking with thoughts of reconciliation. His physical energy is cyclical, determined by his emotional well-being.

Relationship future – Gold star if he meets someone in treatment for love addiction; silver star if he meets someone via the lonely hearts ads.; bronze star if friends trust him enough to introduce him to a mutual acquaintance.

Theme song – 'Don't You Want Me' by The Human League.

Sex rating – Great if he thinks you won't have him back. Not so much effort if you've already given him your spare set of keys.

 9/10   7/10   5/10   9/10

aspects of the type

The Obsessive Lover is the damaged romantic. He could be a former boyfriend, an ex-lover, a fiancé that can't let you go. He's history but he refuses to accept that he has to move on from past relationships to be able to honour those in the future. He will convince himself that he has so much love to give that little else is important. The problem is that he doesn't know where he ends and others begin and this creates situations in which he can easily be hurt.

This guy chooses to live a life swept by great waves of emotion. He knows very clearly the type of woman he can attract. The emphasis are the inevitable consequences. Because he is impulse driven, he finds it hard to work through difficulties. And another aspect of his personality is his inability to voice his wants or needs. He will tell himself that silence is a good way to keep the peace and have an easy life. But he lives in the past, rewinding scenes of conflict and reworking what he could have said or done. The Obsessive Lover wears the mask of denial and delusion, choosing to remain still while the world around him moves on.

Obsessive Lover types are extrovert when attracted to someone. They really do try

> **The Obsessive Lover wears the mask of denial and delusion, choosing to remain still while the world around him moves on.**

he places on idealistic love distorts his vision and he often develops crushes on unavailable people. Someone living in another country, travelling to his city infrequently, would be the perfect choice, offering wonderful opportunities to indulge in romantic fantasy. A chance meeting will initiate the opening scene of his love script, and like some eternal soap opera, the play begins again: same type, different player.

The Obsessive Lover is in an isolated place at the height of his love addiction. Chronically sensitive, melancholic and defensive, he feels the world is against him. Suspicion and paranoia to impress in the early stages of seduction, fast forwarding through a relationship. Don't be surprised if he sends you flowers and takes you to the opera or to Paris for the weekend.

He is a dreamy type who loves to spend as much time as possible with his partner and as little time as possible with himself.

He may be very shy about his past and focus on future events. But this guy is not a mystery; he's an ace manipulator. He wants to be loved and to love. He is the guy at the party who tries to snare you with a lingering, loaded look. He's out there and he's social!

 4/10  2/10

aspects of the soul

The Obsessive Lover journeys through life with a feeling that something is missing. He feels incomplete without the presence of another person with whom to share every experience: life is the glass half empty rather than the glass half full.

This guy is not in tune with his soul. A deeply sensitive individual, his chief need is to understand himself and his complicated emotional map. Although he believes that he has spent a lifetime fulfilling other people's emotional needs, he has in fact created only a sense of loss, a void, within himself. Remember the wisdom in the words, 'No one can ever give to another that which they cannot give themselves'? He may pray constantly at the altar of devotion for his lover never to leave, but he remains disenchanted and confused, unable to understand why he cannot sustain a long-term relationship.

Actually, although he yearns for a passionate and fulfilling union, he is terrified of the thing which he so desperately seeks. Denial has distorted his inner vision, arousing flights of fancy, romantic yearnings and hopes of future partnership, and leaving him ill equipped to handle the responsibility of commitment. He focuses his attention on what is missing in his life and, in comparison, what is available seems unappealing. He will plant the seeds of a relationship in a shallow bed and uproot the seedling to see how the roots are doing, not allowing time for them to grow. Then he panics and creates a drama to act out his fear by becoming smothering, possessive, jealous and envious. And he can't stop repeating this subconscious, destructive pattern of sabotage.

He assumes the stance of the lover longing for his beloved, relishing both the sadness of the loss of love and the romantic anticipation of a perfect future mate. The present remains a rehearsal for the time when his soul will be awakened through love as he sees himself becoming whole and happy. Choosing to ignore the demands of self-realization, he prefers instead the familiarity of sweet melancholy, and the sense of yearning he carries with him takes on the quality of soul searching. Merely a rite of passage for many adolescents as they explore the extremes of emotional life, for the Obsessive Lover this behaviour becomes a pattern that restricts his spiritual growth.

 2/10   5/10

in real life
the emotional vampire

the art of love

The Obsessive Lover is a whirlwind of activity whenever he spots his love. He plots and plans to woo and win. Suddenly it is spring in December and he cannot contain his joy. His obsessive attentions may make the object of his affections feel more like an idol than a person who is recognized, appreciated and loved for herself. Because he is emotionally immature, he expects the same in return, demanding total devotion, undivided attention and constant availability.

Yet once he senses that he has captured his heart's desire, he freaks out. The fear of loss begins to dominate his thoughts and he uses a trial-by-fire method of testing this new love to protect himself from abandonment. So that he can reject before he is rejected, he safeguards from being hurt by changing the emotional climate. Instead of building a firm foundation for intimacy, he decimates any hope of security in the relationship. Time and time again he arrives at this point of crisis, regenerating the cycle of fixation and loss.

To survive in love he follows a dream that promises satisfaction in the future only to find dissatisfaction when he achieves it. He seduces and then rejects, only to re-adopt. 'I didn't know if I loved you until we parted, and then I missed you so much.' This is the Obsessive Lover's life-script. Setting up and playing the emotional distance game – come close, go away – is what he does best, his hallmark. He cherishes people when he wants them and is uncaring, even malicious, when he doesn't. He distances himself as soon as he is needed and craves attention and affection as soon as others want to go away. It is these mixed signals that undermine the trust that anchors a relationship.

Once his ex has moved on, he clings to his memories of past times. Retreating to his memory bank for safety, he crosses the line into self-deception, telling himself that his fantasies of love represent an authentic and intense relationship, now gone, which will be resumed once he wins back his love. He throws caution and self-discipline out of the window as he

reaches for the telephone. Even an answering machine will give him his fix and he plugs into the emotional fantasy he so desperately needs. He warehouses his relationships, hoarding stacks of unfinished business, as he chases unrealistic hopes and dreams of the future.

♥ 3/10   ◉ 3/10

into action / interaction

the hook

Because he's a romantic who is never satisfied with what he's got, dazzle him with your aloofness and indifference. Look like you are not interested in any way. Cold-shoulder him and you will have him hook, line and sinker. This guy gets tense when things seem predictable so don't return his calls, be slow to respond to invitations and keep him guessing. Show off your originality when the moment is right.

into love

Help him to consider the territory that lies between love and hate: to him it is a void without the emotional gratification he is used to running to or from. Try to help him adapt to intimacy by reassuring him about the merits of his connection with you. Try to instill safety in the relationship by encouraging him to relax and live day-to-day, enjoying the small things in life.

out of love

Double check, triple check and then check again: do you really want out? If you do, save yourself and him a lot of heartache and tell him that you want this to be permanent. Don't buy into his sentimentality or his push-me-pull-you intrigues, which will only prolong the agony. Give him as much confidence and honesty as you can and go.

love lesson

One foot in the past and one in the future means zero in the present. Don't get caught in the loop.

inheritor

the archetype: The Innocent, beneficiary of family circumstance, successor, first born

the persona

how he appears to be

How to spot him – At the right hand of his father, working late at the family pizzeria, restoring fences on the family estate, mail dropping for the family business.

Dialogue / Verbal – Regional, urban, suburban, posh, bourgeois ... anything goes.

Chat-line / Pick-up script – 'Do you know how to drive a combine harvester?' 'How many plates can you carry?' 'Are you fertile?'

Life course – To continue the family business.

Accessories – Pocket money, relatives, ever-ready bedroom at home for the no.1 boy, ageing nanny, family crest, family tartan, family apartment on the Costa del Sol.

Day job – Butcher, baker, candlestick maker: jobs range from helping out at the hot-dog stand to leasing the ballroom for corporate conferences. Learns the trade from father. Eager boys inherit the work ethic of a job well done but cash-poor blue-bloods resist being answerable to a boss.

Babe history – Mate-searching starts early. All females are sniffed out, from dud debutantes to local beauty queens; gold-diggers are eliminated. History repeats itself as he marries his parents' favourite.

Theme song – 'My Generation' by The Who.

Fantasy – To meet a babe who knows nothing of his origins and loves him for who he is.

the shadow

who he really is

Bad habits – He works crazy hours. When duty calls, he answers. He doesn't know how to have fun. Forgets your birthday, has little empathy with your world and compares you unfavourably with your mother.

What he doesn't say / Secrets and silences – 'I need an heir. I've been waiting for this all my life. Tradition counts. Blood is thicker than water.'

Hidden agenda – To override any sibling interference. To make hard work look like easy work. To expand what he's been given.

Philosophical mantra – You reap what you sow.

Accessories – Family secrets, mad great aunt, family accountant, pa's pint glass or daddy's hip flask, hand-me-down bespoke suit, home cooking, family motto.

Energy barometer – If he's got to open and close the shop, he'll be too weary to fully enjoy the fruits of his labour. Inheritor types with a 'big egg' sleep with one eye open.

Relationship future – He makes plans; mummy makes dates. This guy is over-protected and may be spoilt. Don't sacrifice your last choccy.

Theme song – 'I Want To Break Free' by Queen.

Sex rating – When the heat is on, he enjoys love under the covers. Sexually he's a stayer, not a stud. He'll want you to sing him a lullaby afterwards!

 3/10   8/10   6/10   7/10

aspects of the type

This guy has been handed something on a plate. But it may not be a ticket to freedom. It may be a ball and chain. Inheritors come in many guises from the boy next door, who inherits his father's pitch at the market, to the royal prince. It's all relative. Instilled in him as a young child is his pre-determined role in life. He is brought up to believe in family ties and he knows only too well that blood is thicker than water.

Whether rich or poor, this type is the focus of intense expectation. He's seen as the lucky one, the boy initiated into manhood by the gift of land, money or the family business. He is under

family circle. Its standards of behaviour will most likely take the place of ideals.

His code of conduct may be key to his choice of partners, for business and for pleasure, and intense focus on his role can lead to an obsessive search for perfection. He is locked into a narcissistic search for a likeness of himself. This mirroring in relationships satisfies his need for security. His survivor persona stems from one of two upbringings: emotional deprivation, perhaps involving boarding school, or passive parenting resulting from mum and dad meeting his every demand.

> **He finds it hard to break from the attitudes characteristic of his family circle. Its standards of behaviour will most likely take the place of ideals.**

pressure to fulfill other people's ideas about who and what he is. Does he have what it takes? Will he put the family's interests first? Can he turn the company around? Will he care for the older members of the clan?

With the package comes an entitlement agenda of the first order. Confident, witty and trained to hold an audience, he's likely to be quick with the compliments, all qualities that score in the dating scene. And his birthright may mean this type has the pick of the crop in any walk of life. But, loyal to family protocol, the Inheritor is wary of outsiders. He finds it hard to break from the attitudes characteristic of his

How the Inheritor hacks his way through these obstacles will make or break him. He may have a period of being unsettled with racy, romantic and scandalous outbreaks acting as a rite of passage to his new responsibilities. Or he may be an anarchist of the privileged class, adopting a no-rules-apply ethic. Some Inheritors, especially cash happy ones, break out in a frenzied spiral of decadence. Destructive as this might be, their journey to freedom and self-discovery represents a form of soul searching. If you're out to ensnare an heir that has long left behind the upper crusties gang, then look to super-happening drinking clubs in grotty areas.

 5/10   4/10

aspects of the soul

The soul of the Inheritor hides behind an exterior that has been moulded and polished by his parents, and maybe for generations before that. He may find it harrowing to make necessary changes and to accept new ways of doing things. To look at life in a different way, to see through the restrictions of the family set-up, will involve rethinking how he can respond to the demands of duty and loyalty with a true sense of responsibility towards himself. And that kind of responsibility just isn't on his list.

The aristocratic man, in particular, will not be influenced by the fleeting visions of new-wave thinking. His belief system is founded on an extraordinary trust in the past and it is confirmed by the predictability of his surroundings. History secures commitment to the group and breaking free from this sub-culture may involve sacrifice.

Aside from the institutions of marriage and religion, the Inheritor is not involved in soul searching. He is at ease with his own spirituality – doubt doesn't occur for him – and he does not recognize the ironies of birthright. Happiness lies simply in the role of the provider.

Being part of a strong family unit has given him a secure base from which to start life. But if he lived a stiff-upper-lip existence, where discipline and correct behaviour were paramount and the definition of family intimacy was privacy and discretion, he may have suppressed any ability to be spontaneous and adopted a limited response to emotional warmth. At the other end of the spectrum, passive parenting may have robbed him of discipline, and a pattern of behaviour develops that manifests in manhood as the 'spoilt brat', demanding rather than asking for what he wants. Whichever scenario applies, expectation has also put such incredible demands on him that he may have become confused and frightened about giving back.

Yet the soul's need for connection with other human beings is strong and so an internal conflict begins, resurfacing to inhibit the Inheritor's love for himself. As a result he may lose out by making the wrong choices for himself.

 5/10   7/10

in real life

the trustafarian, guy who inherits the business or property or title, only child, favourite nephew

the art of love

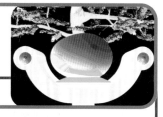

At some stage in his life the Inheritor will be called upon to act for the good of the dynasty. Marriage and parenthood strengthen family ties and resolve inheritance issues so pressure to produce children and be initiated fully into the clan will be strong. This is torment for the man who has not yet decided whether to love the family or leave it.

If he runs from the family, his punishment will be exclusion from the world he knows. But the world of privilege comes at a price. And that price is compromise, however magnificent the package. This man is a link in the genetic chain. Allegiance and shared history force him to choose between what he could do and what he should do. Sadly, for this type there is often a discrepancy between the demands of love and of marriage.

So rule number one: forget the fairytales. He's not a believer. He will probably submit to family pressure to marry a 'suitable' candidate, a partner who appears to be strong, a woman whose close family ties correspond to his own, one that can competently manoeuvre in the clan. A happy ending would mean that he would have to work hard at acquiring self-reliance. But the Inheritor who has been through an isolated childhood looks for people who will take care of him and protect him. After surviving a regimented upbringing, he is attached to a childhood yearning for unconditional love. As this boy became a man, there may have been a sense of disappointment in the nurturing role of his parents and the inevitable result is an enormous loss of self-confidence. As for the 'spoilt brat', constant attention to his needs and wants makes it problematic for him to manoeuvre his way through situations where everything is not exactly as he would like it.

For genuine love to flourish the Inheritor must fight the temptation to remain in these negative situations. Resolution depends on his ability to overcome his sense of entitlement. It is this perspective that leads him into a false sense of security, in which he believes that a perfect life awaits him. He dreams of having a partner whom he wants and who can live up to his family's ideal. If he is lucky, he will find love in 'a suitable marriage'. Destiny and dynasty can sometimes merge successfully and the magic of a true love match can happen. If not, his so-called privilege will be the monkey on his back.

 8/10    4/10

into action / interaction

the hook

Remember that he is rarely alone in a crowd so work your wonder from a distance. Smile, hold his gaze momentarily and then look away. He is attracted to poise, elegance and natural ease. Be passionate about life: this guy never fails to appreciate optimism. If you are really interested, be old school and be modest.

into love

The formula for winning gold stars is to gain trust. Try to give him the confidence to be intuitive with his emotions. But push him too quickly and you'll not be starring in his future. His need to be nurtured can be devoid of subtlety, and he may be used to getting what he wants. Warm his heart gently: a love of music or poetry will soon transform his shyness into sensuality.

out of love

This guy has expectations, not only of you but of himself. Failure in love will most likely mean that he'll respond by rejecting you before you reject him. His chill factor means he knows how to construct a cold front, so don't be surprised if he retaliates with 'don't touch'.

love lesson

Don't spoil him. You're his lover, not his mother.

bohemian

the archetype: The Magician, freedom lover, romantic idealist, intuitive and unorthodox

the persona

how he appears to be

How to spot him – Crossing the street to buy milk in his dressing gown, smoking pot in a Japanese garden at 10am, or happily being a lounge lizard in a secret den of iniquity. And he's the one that looks different in a crowd.

Dialogue / Verbal – Street talk meets lyrical romantic. He speaks with a pronounced accent, one of his own making, and his language is cultivated for his delight only. He loves to hear the words tripping from his tongue before an audience that has to decode his meaning.

Chat-line / Pick-up script – 'Be a troubadour and play my lute.' 'What beautiful eyes you have, Little Red Riding Hood.' 'Have you read the metaphysical poets?' 'Darling, it's your mind I'm in love with.' 'Are you *happening*?'

Life course – To explore and exploit sensuality.

Accessories – Cranky or classic automobile to get around in, first-edition books, stacks of old newspapers, collection of corner chairs, opium stash.

Day job – Trustafarian or just plain poor: being boho is a full-time occupation.

Babe history – Adores and harasses them.

Theme song – 'Love Like Laughter' by Beth Orton.

Fantasy – To be grape fed and fondled at the same time.

the shadow

who he really is

Bad habits – Highly critical: tracks you for imperfections in the way you do mundane, everyday tasks. Gets lost in minutiae, frustrated when you don't do things his way, late for dates and forgets the red wine.

What he doesn't say / Secrets and silences – 'Does my cigarette burn show? It's tiring being a rebel. Please don't break my heart.'

Hidden agenda – To seduce you into his world of words and wisdom, wantonness and waywardness, dreams and delicacies. To use you like a chilli pepper: to season the length of days. To be completely accepted.

Philosophical mantra - Tomorrow, people, is where it's at.

Accessories – Wine, women and non-commercial music, herb garden, used breadboard and peanut butter knife, stolen ash trays, late nights, hand-me-down clothes.

Energy barometer – Like a snake in the grass, his belly not touching the ground, this guy will drop in for the Big Chill.

Relationship future – Fashion some invisible reins and ride the tiger bareback for the pleasure trip of a lifetime.

Theme song – 'Water From A Vine Leaf' by William Orbit.

Sex rating – Very little sex on the run: this guy wants to take his time. He'll boho you!

 4/10　 3/10　 9/10　 6/10

aspects of the type

The Bohemian is unconventional in thought, word and deed. His avant-garde approach originates in his instinctive objective to define himself as a person apart from the whole, and he is very at ease with his uniqueness. The need to be outrageously different in everything he does have only one mirror at home but this doesn't mean that he's without insecurities. Socially he shines in his own particular limelight. He loves to be where it's at. But it must be in a way that allows him to feel secure: he wants to feel that people look to him for direction. And they do.

His experience of day-to-day life appears to be more thoughtful than other people's.

is fundamental and so is informality. Watch him in action and you'll find that he improvises his fluid, ever-changing identity – considering every experience the world has to offer and reacting to it spontaneously, the only preconception being that his response must be different. His experience of day-to-day life appears to be more thoughtful than other people's. For him, every second seems to count. He appears to do everything with a certain mindfulness, a certain pace. If he is making tea or coffee, you can be sure it is jasmine tea or freshly ground coffee. No milk – it would kill the taste. And taste is where it's at for the Bohemian.

Inevitably the guy will be involved in bizarre antics whenever his free will takes off on a wild escapade, but his absurdity is absolutely spontaneous. There is nothing premeditated about this type. And that is why he is special. He is vain, but his vanity is prompted externally rather than internally. It is when he finds himself pursued by others that he begins to recognize and relish in his own attractiveness. He may

This type is appreciated by those who share the vision and those who aspire to be as independent in thought as he is. He is wonderful in a group or one-on-one. Being a talented observer, he doesn't miss a thing.

Idiosyncrasies are one a penny with this guy, who will appeal to the freak in you. Exoticism is his hallmark. But there is a downside to his drive to be different and that's his extreme unpredictability. Rebelliousness shapes his emotional life: he can be erratic, selfish and stubborn. He switches from caring to caustic and back again. And he may have an impeccable memory, able to recall the good and the bad, the praise and the put-downs.

The Bohemian is largely non-acquisitional, but he surrounds himself with a few carefully chosen objects that reflect his need for a life rich in cultural references. He will also involve himself in subterranean cultures that advocate off-the-wall attitudes. This type lives on the edge of society: never quite in the system and yet never quite outside it.

 6/10   6/10

aspects of the soul

The evolved Bohemian is a complete fatalist. His attitude towards life is largely based on optimism: he flies by the seat of his pants. This guy has recognized the role that chance plays in the events that have marked his life and gives due importance to it – he has learnt one of the essential lessons of earthly existence. The less experienced and perhaps younger type will still struggle with life's inconsistencies and variables.

The Bohemian has to defend his individuality in a world that caters for the majority. He must deal with pressure from others to fit their perceptions of how he should be. Because his values and ethics may be more difficult to accept than his persona, he may become used to justifying his personal philosophy. And nobody can justify his life like this guy. He has taken great care to shape his response.

He likes to think of himself as a complex character. He wants to be seen as self-confident, making life choices that will set him apart from the rest, disregarding the rules and regulations that define mainstream contemporary culture and questioning linear thinking. But he also projects himself as contemplative, concerned with honouring the soul's impulse, someone who chews over the meaning of life. In fact, he is incredibly laidback, more intent on carrying himself off in an effortless display of style than anything else. Spiritually he feels free, not bound by any obligation to behave in a particular way.

However, he is sensitive and intuitive, and he knows what he values. Pleasure is his starting point. All that is languid, luxurious and romantic is hugely significant to him. The password to his psyche is reverence. He likes to give back to the world and often does so by making a gift of his vivid and sensual imagination.

In not belonging completely to the ordered, everyday world, the Bohemian affirms his convictions. And, by being true to himself, he creates a place to belong, his place in the sun. This man is an outstanding example of individual strength grounded in personal belief.

 4/10   5/10

in real life

the ageing hippie, llama breeder, social drop-out, artiste, story teller, muse

the art of love

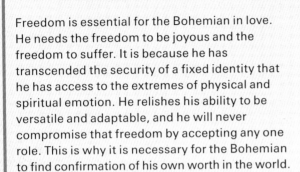

Freedom is essential for the Bohemian in love. He needs the freedom to be joyous and the freedom to suffer. It is because he has transcended the security of a fixed identity that he has access to the extremes of physical and spiritual emotion. He relishes his ability to be versatile and adaptable, and he will never compromise that freedom by accepting any one role. This is why it is necessary for the Bohemian to find confirmation of his own worth in the world.

Sadly he does not always take into consideration the feelings of those around him. He likes to think that he knows best and finds it almost impossible to admit defeat, or recognize his own stubbornness. Because he'll never compromise who he is, he becomes self-protective if he feels he is being compartmentalized. So arrogance and industrial-strength defensiveness can sour his ability to love. He is the square peg in the round hole, and he won't be changing. He'll risk losing out on love rather than be defeated. This is the hardest thing a partner has to accept. Remember that being 'different from the norm' is isolating, but it can also be inspiring.

With such choice in the personality box, the Bohemian can aim at any number of love targets. He may be an incomparable flirt, and he loves to play. To bring chaos when there is calm and calm when there is chaos. But, although he plays with hearts, he is secretly searching for a mate. This type wants inspiration and passion. He is looking for someone who can match his zest for life.

A declaration of love from the Bohemian is to be trusted. He has invested so much of his time in the search for what is real for him that when he finds it he knows it. He will give his all to creating a safe haven for love to grow. He will respect and respond to his partner's expressions of affection, reciprocating smile for smile, kiss for kiss, caress for caress. This spells a sweet formula for love with all its opportunities to trust, to risk and to share.

But if it's you he's got his eagle eye on, watch out. High maintenance is an understatement. The cost of upkeep on an eccentric is enormous; in fact, it is never-ending. As rewarding as he is, with his unique angle on life and his opinions on how to live it, he'll test your patience. Because he is so romantically involved, he will be irritated by what he perceives as your imperfections and he will demand that you comply with his quirky standards of etiquette. His romanticism cannot conquer futility. It should, but hey! everyone's human.

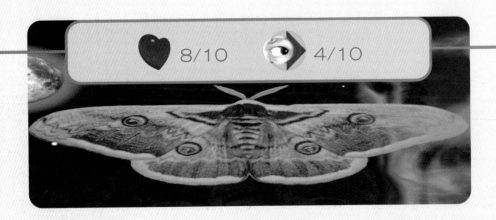

❤ 8/10   👁▶ 4/10

into action / interaction

the hook

Be direct if you want this guy to notice you. Act cool but not indifferent. Dare to be different. Be street *and* wise. Look like you are someone who adores life and doesn't mind sharing the secret. Captivate him with your uncompromising gaze – who dares wins – and then tease him with your lightness and humour.

into love

Strengthen the relationship by being sensitive to his vulnerability when he opens up and lets you in. Be willing to embrace his vision of the future, but keep your own identity on track. Create together. Take him with a pinch of salt. When he spits the dummy, don't react to his outbursts. He'll only feel more insecure. Leave the room and allow him to cool down in his own time. He is wonderful, and he'll amaze you with his stimulating perspectives.

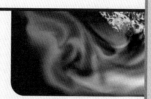

out of love
Cramp his style.

love lesson
Dare to live.

fashion luvvie

the archetype: The Magician, style warrior, beauty freak, king of cool

the persona

how he appears to be

How to spot him – Easy. He relishes his role as the people pleaser. He works the crowd as if he shared past lives with each and every one. Kiss kiss, hug hug, next ...

Dialogue / Verbal – Fashion speak: colour, shape and cut leave little room for politics and philosophy. Trivial is this guy's middle name. But who cares? The latest gossip is who's zooming who.

Chat-line / Pick-up script – 'Are you old enough to be a celebrity?' 'You look just like my new discovery. Turn to the light so I can see your profile .. aah, divine.' 'Do you have a brother?'

Life course – I don't *do* fashion. It's a way of life.

Accessories – Measuring tape, dress pins, sketch-pad, library of costume design, black T-shirt, sushi, passport, portfolio, Polaroid film.

Day job – Fashion designer, fashion photographer, fashion editor, hair and make-up stylist, runway choreographer, model.

Babe history – Swinger with the celebs. Incestuous as it is, the past is a mystery. Hates being labelled straight or gay so presume he's both. Don't think numbers.

Theme song – 'The Model' by Kraftwerk.

Fantasy – Dressing up to be undressed at a cross-dressing orgy entitled 'Glamourama' in some Italian palazzo.

the shadow

who he really is

Bad habits – Sucks you in and spits you out, sticks the knife in as soon as your back is turned and pouts when he doesn't get his own way.

What he doesn't say / Secrets and silences – 'I don't like you but you're necessary. Sweetie, that colour just doesn't do you any favours. Don't outshine me.'

Hidden agenda – To gain gold stars from the movers and the shakers of his world. To further his career at all costs; to annihilate competition.

Philosophical mantra – You're only as good as your last show.

Accessories – Valium for supersonic stress, kava-kava for organic balancing, designer drugs, lawyer to deal with cases of unfair dismissal, trailer-park mum to sign autographs when he's not around.

Energy barometer – This guy is like a yo-yo: the highest of highs and the lowest of lows. His attention (when it's on you) is overwhelming, his eye for detail exhausting.

Relationship future – If he casts you, there will be memorable moments. But will he want to share the limelight?

Theme song – 'You're So Vain' by Carly Simon.

Sex Rating – Mostly sex-on-the-run stuff, contrasting with those few stolen moments when he relaxes into romanticism.

 2/10   3/10 5/10   9/10

aspects of the type

Welcome to the world of the dream merchant. Welcome to the world of here and now. Many are called, but few are chosen. This type is a creative visionary. He oozes inspiration. He has attitude. Any publicity is good publicity. Camera shy? Oooh, never. He's always ready for the close-up. This gregarious drama queen exudes far too much star quality to be in the mere mortals category. He lives every moment as though it were a self-made documentary entitled *My Life*. Open his Pandora's box and you'll find the missing link to his past. This is a man concerned with moving from the back row to the front seat. He aspires to be king of the heap with the limelight bouncing off the walls.

He is his own creation from what has been done before to what will be done again. Forget café society: this guy is searching for what's new, what's happening. He knows what's hot and what's not; what's to die for and what's dead. This man of the moment is directional; where he goes others will follow. He'll take us to places we've never been and in return he demands status and professional recognition.

The successful Fashion Luvvie will be chameleon-like or possess the timelessness of Sublime Style. He dresses either in many robes or just one. He is an ace manipulator, a skill learnt in the jungle of egos. His own inflated ego means he likes to play, and in that sense he

retains a youthful spirit. There is a side to this type which embraces deception – he can be almost Machiavellian in performance. Unscrupulous and deceitful, his methods of persuasion secure the fashion-mag editorial splash. He will walk over the dead to get what he wants. But he is not a talented negotiator because his concern for detail drives him into perfectionist mode. In the workplace he is happy to delegate chores while demanding the best.

Creativity for king cool is the mother of invention. His personality is fluid, always changing, adapting to match his current

> **His personality is fluid, always changing, adapting to match his current obsession.**

obsession. His craving for stimulation and inspiration may make him the slave of hype. His feminine aspect is directed towards the construction of a celebrity identity. Being part of the fashion *cognoscenti* means he must constantly update his profile. Right here, right now. Life on the knife-edge is fun fuelled by adrenaline. Inspiration is taken from his latest muse. He or she is then brought into the inner circle. The Fashion Luvvie lives only in the actualization of his own fantasies, and the kick is his ability to merge the real with the unreal. Stealing beauty is a full-time occupation.

 5/10   8/10

aspects of the soul

His perception of adventure leads him to explore the field of dreams. Superficial as those dreams might be, satisfaction takes him to a place of self-confidence and 'superdom'. Fashion is his passion and it fulfils him, as does the adoration he grabs from his audience. At best he can gain iconic status. But, as the fables say, all that glitters is not gold. The world of fantasy can hinder the journey of this type by bringing him into self-neglect. The desire for fame and fortune denies him a more intimate understanding of himself, creating conflict between the worlds of futility and substance. In revealing only his external persona, the Fashion Luvvie is defined by what he looks like and how well he presents.

It is the creative aspect of his personality that gives a window into his heart and soul. Should you have a chance to see him in action, watch carefully from the sidelines. What he sees as beauty is pivotal to an understanding of how he views his world. Through beauty he is able to combine those qualities that delight the mind and the senses. It is in the weaving together of sources of inspiration that he demonstrates his ability to take what he needs from the outside world and reinterpret it in his own way. He gives new meaning to contemporary culture. By delving into the past, he reworks and originates the images of lifestyle, predicting who we will be, how we will live and what we will wear tomorrow.

His self-worth appears to be intact, but the need for constant approval is what motivates this type. He values himself through the regard of others, like an orphan, full of wide-eyed innocence and wonderment, always surprised and delighted by encouragement. In living the life of the Fashion Luvvie, he feels part of a family or collective, mingling with many different faces, many different tribes, accepted for his non-conformist, perhaps even rebellious, nature.

 3/10   2/10

in real life

the shopaholic, fashion victim, fashion police, fashion-mag subscriber

the art of love

Ah love, aah romance, aaah dinner *à deux*. Music, lights, camera, action. The art of loving for the Fashion Luvvie is pure drama. Everything must be just right; every detail attended to. Wooing needs its pleasure dome: it's the perfect excuse for creating occasion. He will swoon at your moon; be the laughter to your joke. Romance will go off the scale if he lets it. His heart craves adventure. He is ready and willing to blast off into the orbit of that utopia where dreams can be played out, where air kissing becomes mouth to mouth.

His operatic sensitivities make him the mikado of love. He idolizes what he sees as pure, but he needs a partner who delights in sensual pleasure as much as he does. A dangerous liaison will entice him no end: 'I love it, I want it, and I have to have it.' It is hard for this guy to settle for any one thing. He is a collector. Predictably, any object of desire must look good – big smile, eyes and teeth. Way out is your way in. The drawback to his world is your sell-by-date. This guy has a thirst for the unexposed and unexplored. He will want to conquer the affections of his wandering eye. Always on the lookout, glancing over your shoulder, he scans the horizon. Unless completely swept off his feet, his commitment to love is temporary.

To reveal his softer, more human side, the Fashion Luvvie will have to abandon his self-generated life drama. Exaggerated moments of flamboyance will eventually have to be limited if he really wants to be authentic, to share his intimate fears and emotions with another person. But being quiet and away from the pressure of professional demands may be a rarity. When the season heats up, his schedule demands a 24-hour day and his short fuse will blow from time to time. Temper tantrums and hissy fits are part of the way he handles high anxiety. Be warned: he doesn't realize his capacity to wound deeply. Once he has been angry, he recovers quickly. He gets over it and gets on with it. Because he is magnetic he will keep you coming back for more, but you in turn must be strong enough to deal with challenging times as he fades from the limelight.

4/10   7/10

into action / interaction

the hook

Be a shining star: flirt from afar. Win him by being mysterious and shy. Don't do labels. You must have natural style and above all carry yourself well. Relax – don't push it. But know the deal if you want to enter this guy's world. You're there to bolster his reputation. Once you have caught him unawares with seductive, playful charm, make sure you let him know you're up for fantasy in dreamtime. Whatever you do, don't compete.

into love

When an invitation to intimacy is accepted, move quickly to satisfy his inquisitiveness. He has high energy and you will have to work at being constantly in tune with his inspirational side. The best way to do this is to make yourself his inspiration. Be spontaneous with your affections. He needs first-hand experience of who you are to ground a relationship. It is this sense of deep and genuine exchange that he lacks in his superficial, one-dimensional world of acquaintance.

out of love

If you feel the need to spread your wings and fly, don't choose a passive approach and steer clear of provoking careless whispers. As a people-pleaser, his façade and self-image will inevitably be damaged if he feels that he is the one left behind. Tread carefully and allow him to have a knee-jerk reaction. This may be vengeful. Let him accept the change of circumstances: don't reassure him or wrap him up in cotton wool. He is a survivor and can bounce back, taking with him the best of your time together.

love lesson

Give him a sense of full-time love while you live in the magic of the moment.

zen man

the archetype: The Altruist, seer, medium who sees all sides of the question

the persona

how he appears to be

How to spot him – At the gathering, in an aura of love, compassion and happiness. Seated under the bodhi tree, the man with the luminous glow.

Dialogue / Verbal – Simplicity, clarity, authenticity: he listens more than he speaks.

Chat-line / Pick-up script – 'When the pupil is ready, the master will come.'

Life course – To make the world a better place.

Accessories – Gong, prayer mat, candle.

Day job – Guru, monk, priest, spiritual adviser or teacher, white wizard, modern-day mystic.

Babe history – Vow of silence.

Theme song – 'Natural Mystic' by Bob Marley.

Fantasy – Two become one.

the shadow

who he really is

Bad habits – He is too kind, too truthful and not always available.

What he doesn't say / Secrets and silences – 'Wake up! I'm human and I need to love too.'

Hidden agenda – Doesn't have one.

Philosophical mantra – Cultivate loving kindness.

Accessories – None.

Energy barometer – Saved for opening the third eye and restoring self-love.

Relationship future – He's expecting his Beloved any minute.

Theme song – 'Spiritual Love' by Urban Species.

Sex rating – He's a semi-realized tantric master.

 1/10 9/10  10/10 1/10

aspects of the type

The Zen Man is the ascetic. He lives a non-toxic life, abstaining from anything that is not good for him: alcohol, cigarettes, caffeine, recreational drugs, casual sex. He exists within the world but is not part of it, accepting his place as a helper and a giver. He is characterized by his state of oneness with the Divine – a condition he experiences through mysticism, revelation or deep feelings of joy and contentment.

This fully fledged member of planet earth is mindful of everything he does. His motivation is to restore harmony in a confused world and he takes care not to inflict harm on other people.

people see him. He is relaxed and happy in his own company. This man has accepted himself and confronted his reasons for existence. Direct, assertive and ethical, the Zen Man is full of laughter. He is the ultimate harmonizer, regularly called upon to smooth out misunderstandings between his friends.

This type loves an early start. He wakes up feeling fresh as a daisy and prepares himself for the day by doing some tai chi, chi gong, yoga, pilates or any of the fashionable eastern body-work techniques that he has studied over the years. Then he has his quiet time, either sitting

He is characterized by his state of oneness with the Divine.

He is a wise person who is thoughtful and respectful. He is not tempted in any way to become richer or to better his social standing. Celebrity isn't what he's after either; he steers clear of any semblance of falseness.

The Zen Man is a private man but he hides away only when he needs to recharge his energy. He is not unreachable and may even be a social butterfly. He loves the company of others and will not turn down an invitation. A great participator, this type is funny without being cruel, loving without being patronizing, and honest without being superior.

His freedom from fear and his magnetic personality make him attractive to almost everyone and he has zero anxiety about how

in meditation or visualizing mandalas to inspire stillness of the mind. Next he juices his favourite combination of carrot, celery, ginger and apple to give himself a vitality boost. For him, every day is a new beginning.

The man does have flaws, but compared to those of any other type they are almost unnoticeable. Kindness is his hallmark and his patience is never-ending. He books in advance for a string of extracurricular activities, including retreats, peace festivals, green gatherings and sweat lodges. He will be a singularly calm person among the throng of excitable enthusiasts. What separates the Zen Man from all other types is that he lives in the here and now. When he speaks to you, he will be present. What a joy!

 7/10 9/10

aspects of the soul

The Zen Man is an evolved being. He has seen his immortality. Unafraid of death, he has become the light that guides others in their journey towards a higher consciousness. Defined by his commitment to a spiritual way of life, he feels that the world needs him to carry the message of love and peace. He may be an initiate of a religious or spiritual organization but this is not essential.

The Zen Man's soul is magnificent. Like a reed of compelling beauty springing from the swamp, it cannot be ignored. This guy has experienced transformation of the psyche and the spirit – a feat that many people see as unrealistic or unnecessary. He has examined his life and changed it by abandoning old attitudes and karmic patterns. He is rigorous in his spiritual maintenance, cleansing his being by attempting to purge impurities and by burning up his negativities. And on his stomping ground of the earthly plane, he has learnt life's lessons, growing through adversity to advance further along the path of enlightenment. It takes discipline and perseverance to sacrifice aspects of oneself but his soul is in such good nick because he has remained true to his purpose.

He stays clear of any practice that would encourage pride and ego. Either would interrupt his inner voice and contaminate all the purification he has undergone. But he never stands still in the process of change – he believes that truth is found by living. He remains constantly open to experience, allowing himself to feel his feelings and then move through them.

He has compassion for all sentient beings, believing that all plant life, all animal life and all human life has a soul. This makes him great to be around. Communication with him is easy because he is easy on himself. He has put the mind games, the insecurities and the harshness aside and welcomed love as his mentor.

This type is perceptive and he has the power of healing. It is his intense self-examination that helps him to empathize with and tolerate other people's character defects and projections, and his experience of change draws others to him. Using his great advisory skills, he is able to initiate positive transformation. Never overwhelmed by hardship, he has the maturity to find opportunity in whatever life has to offer each and every one of us.

 10/10   9/10

in real life

the philanthropist, author of meditation books, self-styled guru and circuit speaker, guy with twenty godchildren

the art of love

The Zen Man is the catch of the century. He is radiant and his internal fire attracts lovers like moths to a light. To him, love is the universal order. He needs to love and he needs to be loved. He aspires to the noblest ideal of love – a state in which he can share everything with another.

Being in love with a Zen Man is the opportunity to realize unconditional love and comfort. He embraces life compassionately, building an impregnable empire of emotional strength and clarity. When he hears the cry of the human heart, he will answer with gentleness and common sense. This is not a guy who will take you for a ride just to make him feel like a man. He is the sustainer, not the thief, of many hearts. His attributes make him appealing to women who are looking for a complete man. Such gems are rare and, surprisingly enough, are seen by some women as just too nice.

He is looking for someone who can give as well as take. He is a good judge of character and will make a decision based on his pure heart. If the Zen Man's eyes are cast in your direction, he will see you as a blossom on a tree and await the ripening of the fruit. He is not pushy in love and will be eager not to scare you away with his depth of feeling.

His faith in the power of love is profound and in matters of love he puts all his eggs in one basket. But he recognizes that there are obstacles that make it difficult for each of us to love. He has learnt to honour the wounds of his heart, and he will use the relationship to learn more about himself as well as you.

The biggest plus is the Zen Man's non-judgmental disposition. He will nurture and support you in your hour of need. In return, you must take responsibility for your own actions. There's no hiding how you really feel with this guy – he wasn't born yesterday. And don't suppose, just because he is a semi-realized tantric master, that he will put up with anything! Far from it. The Zen Man can spot emotional blackmail at twenty paces. He will confront you if he catches you out and pull you back on track. In this way he practises integrity – he demands an honest exchange between two souls and hopes for synergy. If he falls in love with you, he will shower you with rose petals, attending to your every need. His intention is to give without expecting anything in return but even the most evolved of Zen Men may stumble.

He is the ideal lover because he embraces the polarities of his feminine and masculine energies so completely. Sexually this makes for a great time. If you fit, he will expect you to bring a magic of your own and he will want to experience the full extent of your sexuality, cherishing each touch, moment by moment. Don't be shy of seeking new horizons with him. The most important thing to bear in mind is that you may only have one chance.

9/10   1/10

into action / interaction

the hook

Don't rush it: build a friendship first and see where this takes you. Be balanced. Show that you have an innate integrity. Then increase the intensity by spending more time together. Flirt with your Zen Man by entering into his personal space gently and sensitively. Refine your come-hither look.

into love

The Zen Man's main concern is whether you can live in harmony, like the sun and the moon. But he will not compromise his way of living. His hope is that you enjoy what he has to offer. Try not to interrupt his life and don't move in until you've been through all the seasons as a couple. Respect his need for calm, pursue your own interests and become a vegan.

out of love

If he wants to swap your couch for a bed of nails, ask him to join you for rest and recreation away from home before he makes a decision. If he is evolving into a crashing bore, give him a pep talk of his own and pray for him as you exit from the love nest. Stay friends.

love lesson

Try not to look for proof or reasons if he tells you that he loves you. He just does.

acknowledgments

We are indebted to each other for a rewarding partnership which has taught us humility, grace and fearlessness. Thanks to the full moon in Scorpio and for the laughter that gave this book life. Thanks to all the people whose help and dedication made writing this book possible. To everybody who gave us the support we needed. To Griselda Laroche and her kitchen table, which definitely has a power of its own. To Lisha Spar, our agent, who believed in us from the start.

Thank you to Gerard Cunningham for getting us started and for taking a risk. To Nathan Gelber for teaching us that furniture was more important than shoes. To Raffik Brodie for your talent and time spent on our words. Thanks to Martin Lloyd-Elliott and to Mary Vango for their generosity.

Thanks to all the staff at Quadrille for their never-ending enthusiasm and direction; to Alison Cathie, Anne Furniss and Mary Evans for their integrity, guidance and flexibility; to Richard Rockwood and Ben Owen for their creative expertise; to Lawrence Morton for inspiration and advice; to Jo Barnes, Jim Smith, Emma Noble and Helen Desmond; to our editor Mary Davies for her keen understanding and for going that extra mile. Thanks to all the men and women who participated in the research for this book.

Thanks to Dotty Irving and Melody Odusanya at Colman Getty; to Jenny Halpen, Helena Saddler and Jo Melzak at Halpen Associates; to Sidonie Schoeff at Joseph; to The Pink House for its blessing; to Heather Reynolds and Erica Spellman in New York; to Tim Motion for his wonderful photography; and to Stephen Tungay at The Color Company who prioritized our proposal.

Thanks to our friends for their unwavering support: Susie Biddu, Kam Gi Chak, Henrietta Palmer, Mathilda Bowan, Jenny Wood, Karima Olokun-Ola, Kathleen Scott, Mia Flodquist, Bev Corlete, Anne Macalpine-Leny, Avtarjeet Dhanjal, Romina Marshall, Alain Yewall, Bisi Lalemi, Diane Schwartz, Vismaya Jeager, Gordon and Claire Barnes and James Lo. You are all shining stars. Thanks to our families with heartfelt appreciation.

And finally to all the men everywhere who rock girls' worlds!

First published in 2000 by
Quadrille Publishing Limited
Alhambra House
27–31 Charing Cross Road
London WC2H OLS

© Text Elizabeth Hearn and Sada Walkington 2000
© Illustrations, design and layout Quadrille Publishing
   Limited 2000

The moral right of the authors has been asserted.

All illustrations by Richard Rockwood except pages 16, 64, 76, 100, 106 by Ben Owen. Special thanks to Adrian Nicholas and Olav Zipser for allowing us to use Adrian's image and Olav's photograph in the Joy Junkie illustration.

Publishing Director: Anne Furniss
Creative Director: Mary Evans
Designer: Richard Rockwood
Assistant Designer: Jim Smith
Copy Editor: Mary Davies
Editorial Assistants: Helen Desmond, Emma Noble
Production: Julie Hadingham, Sarah Tucker, Vincent Smith

British Library Cataloguing in Publication Data
A catalogue record for this book is available from the
British Library.

ISBN 1 902757 51 3

Printed and bound in Italy by Arnoldo Mondadori Spa, Verona.